The Missing Son
A Faroe Island Saga

Copyright © 2010 Jennifer Henke
All rights reserved.

ISBN: 1450560156
EAN-13: 9781450560153
LCCN: 2010901477

The Missing Son
A Faroe Island Saga

Jennifer Henke

Foreword

Jennifer Henke was born in San Francisco and has lived most of her life in the San Francisco Bay Area. She has always enjoyed travelling, and as the youngest in a family of eight children, she often traveled around the U.S. to visit her brothers and sisters. However, it wasn't until her own children were grown and out of college that she took the trip of a lifetime, to a place she had always dreamed of visiting – the Faroe Islands, her father's homeland.

After her first visit to the Faroe Islands in 1997, she returned several times in the next few years with members of her family. Jennifer documented these early visits in long letters to her siblings, accompanied by photos. These letters became the inspiration for this book, when she learned that all of her siblings saved the letters and photos and shared them with family, friends, and co-workers.

In 2005, Jennifer retired from her job as a computer programmer at the Medical Center of the University of California in San Francisco, and spent the following year living in Fuglafjørður, Faroe Islands – her father's home town. During this time, she began documenting her experiences and the beautiful scenery in the Faroe Islands on her web site, www.jenniferhenke.com. She also worked on putting together a book of paintings by one of her relatives, *Mótljós / Into the Light* by Heðin Kambsdal, published in November 2007 in both English and Faroese.

v

One year later, in November 2008, Jennifer published her own book in the Faroe Islands in the Faroese language, *Saknaði Sonurin* (The Missing Son), which tells about her experiences in the Faroe Islands and her discovery her father's family and his homeland. At long last, she is delighted to have her story and her father's history available in English.

Table of Contents

Chapter

1   A Journey into the Past   1
Finding my father's family in the Faroe Islands eighty years after he left home as a young sailor.

2   Fuglafjørður History   17
A short history of my father's family and his home town.

3   Letters from the War Years, 1917-1919   29
Letters to my father from his parents, sister, and two brothers.

4   Welcome   43
The warm welcome given me by my new-found family during my first few days in the Faroe Islands.

5   Letters, 1920–1924   57
The last letters to my father from his family in the Faroe Islands.

6   Getting Acquainted   81
Getting to know my cousins and seeing the spectacular Faroe Islands.

THE MISSING SON — A FAROE ISLAND SAGA

7   Love Letters   95
A surprising love story – letters from my father's fiancée in the Faroe Islands.

8   Celebration and Farewell   117
The annual town festival and my last few days with my cousins.

9   An Able-bodied Seaman   133
My father's stories from his sailing days.

10   Returning to the Faroe Islands   147
Return visits to the Faroe Islands with my brother and my husband.

11   The Next Generation   165
My children visit the Faroe Islands.

12   The Last Love Letters   177
The final love letters from my father's fiancée.

13   Epilogue   197
The end of the story.

Appendices

I   Sailing Records for Hans Jacobsen   203

II   Jacobsen Family Tree   209

List of Photographs

Fuglafjørður bay and mountains	cover
Map of the Faroe Islands	xi
Faroe Islands from the air	xii
Tinganes in Tórshavn	6
Fuglafjørður bay and mountains	12
Fuglafjørður marina	18
Jonathan Henke and museum sleeping cupboards	21
Johannes and Margretha Jacobsen	26
Malene Hansen as a young woman	32
Klaksvík on Borðoy	40
Funningur on Eysturoy	49
Gjógv natural harbor	51
Joen Jacobsen and family	54
Hans Jacobsen in 1923	70
Malene Hansen and Poul Jacob at his confirmation	73
Sheep beside the road	76
Magnus Cathedral in Kirkjubøur	87
Farmhouse in Kirkjubøur	88

Viking houses in Húsavík	90
Tiny wild orchid	93
Crew of ship Guri	102
Fuglafjørður in winter	112
Cousins in Fuglafjørður	121
Vestmanna bird cliffs	123
Ship S/S Bearport	128
Hans Jacobsen in uniform, 1923	140
Island/rock of Tindholmur	142
Waterfall from Saksun museum	148
Peter Jacobsen photographing Tjørnuvík	150
Puffins overlooking Mykines	152
Fuglafjørður beach	160
Satellite dish and drying fish	168
Puffin with fish	171
Waterfall in Fuglafjørður	174
Maren, my father's fiancée	188
Hans Jacobsen with 1929 Chevrolet	192

Map of the Faroe Islands, used by permission, Føroya Myndasavn. ➤

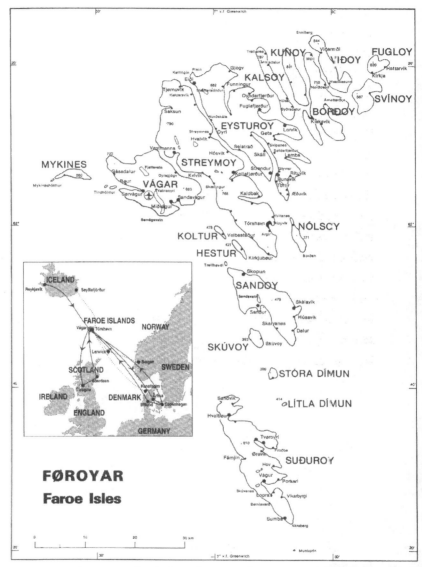

OVERLEAF: *Faroe Islands from the air, with Streymoy in the foreground, and Eysturoy and the northern islands of Kalsoy, Kunoy, and Viðoy in the distance.* ➤

I

My Father's Homeland

Færöerne,   *my father's land,*
almost lost in northern seas,
beyond oceans and continents,
islands mysterious and ancient.

Fuglefjord,   *word in foreign script,*
faded ink on yellowed paper,
crumbling with age.
Reminders of another life, another time,
another world, never quite forgotten.

Faroe.   *Clouds part, revealing hills and bays,*
jagged peaks and valleys,
steep cliffs, shadows fading into mists,
sounds of bird and sea.
Soft grass, each hill a different green,
ever changed in sun and rain and wind.

Faroe.   *The past and present meet*
to make a bridge across the years and oceans.
My father's family is my own,
and I am welcomed as a long lost child.

Føroyar,   *country of my father's birth.*
Føroyar,   *islands where my heart belongs.*

July 7, 1997

Chapter 1 – A Journey into the Past

For the last leg of my flight I made sure I had a seat by the window. During the two hour trip from Copenhagen to the Faroe Islands we flew over clouds and more clouds, with a rare glimpse of deep-blue ocean far below.

"Please fasten seat belts." The announcement was in four languages – Danish, Faroese, German, and English. English was always last. The plane descended through dense clouds, darkening the cabin. Like shadows through the fog, I saw sheer cliffs, then green hills, a narrow bay, a few small villages, and finally a very small airport. After years and years of wondering about these remote islands, I had finally arrived in my father's homeland, all alone and unannounced.

In my luggage I carried a packet of letters that I hoped would help me find out about my father's family. The letters were dated from 1917 to 1924, and each included the town of Fuglefjord on the dateline. They were in Danish, which I couldn't read; but several had been translated. One of these letters included a name that I hoped would be a link to the past, a new baby named Poul Jacob Hansen, born to my father's sister in 1922.

Hans Nils Peter Sofus Jacobsen, my father, was born in the Faroe Islands in 1896, the youngest of seven children. He grew up in the town of Fuglefjord, and like most young men, started sailing full time at about age 14 or 15. During the next 14 or 15 years he sailed all over the world, finally settling permanently in San Francisco. My knowledge of his early life was very sketchy, and he didn't talk much about his past. I could find the Faroe Islands on the map, and I knew that they belonged to Denmark. I also had a sheet of paper listing the names of my father's parents and his brothers and sisters, but more information was hard to come by.

As a child I had asked my father questions about his childhood home, but the answers were always very short. "Was it cold in the winter?" "Yes, but not too cold." ... "Did it snow a lot?" "Sometimes." ... "Did you sail in boats around the island?" "Of course, everyone did." ... "Can you still speak Danish?" "Oh no, I've forgotten it." Eventually I stopped asking questions, but I never stopped wondering what the Faroe Islands were like and whether I still had relatives there.

After my father's death in 1979, we discovered old letters that he had received during his years of sailing, along with photographs, post cards, and sailing records. The letters seemed to be in Danish, and many of them were from his parents, brothers, and sister. We had a few of them translated, but the translations were difficult and awkward since the language was an old-fashioned form of Danish. The letters were set aside, but not forgotten. It seemed that the only way to learn more about my father's homeland and his family was to go to the Faroe Islands. However, with my husband in graduate school and with two small children, such a trip would have to wait.

Eighteen years later, when our youngest child was graduating from college, we decided to splurge and take a "real" vacation. My first choice was a trip to the Faroe Islands. In preparation for the trip we searched the extensive libraries of the University of California in Berkeley, for books that even mentioned the Faroe Islands. We found seven of them, and five of these were very old books about Greenland and Iceland, with a brief chapter on the Faroe Islands. Eventually we located web sites with more practical information, such as airline schedules, hotel listings, and current descriptions of the islands.

The Faroe Islands are a group of 18 small islands in the North Atlantic Ocean, midway between Iceland, Scotland, and Norway, just south of the Arctic Circle. They have a population of about 49,000

A JOURNEY INTO THE PAST

people and 80,000 sheep. In fact the Danish name, Færöerne, means "sheep islands." Tórshavn (population 18,000) is the capital city, located on the island of Streymoy. Fuglafjørður (population 1600) is on the island of Eysturoy. These two large islands are centrally located, and together they are considered the mainland. Since the Second World War, the Faroe Islands have had home rule in the Danish kingdom. Danish had been the only written language when my father was growing up, but with independent home rule, the Faroese language became the standard. This accounted for the differences in spelling between my father's letters and the current tourist literature; the town of Fuglefjord changed to Fuglafjørður and Færöerne became Føroyar (Faroe Islands).

When summer finally arrived, my husband was unable to travel due to a recent illness, but he encouraged me to go alone. Since I could find no hotel in Fuglafjørður in the tourist literature, I made reservations at Hotel Eiði on the northern tip of the island of Eysturoy.

I left San Francisco very early on Tuesday morning, June 24, 1997, flying to Frankfurt and Copenhagen, finally arriving in the Faroe Islands on Wednesday just after noon. I had assumed that the airport would be near the capital city of Tórshavn, but after I arrived I realized that we were on the island of Vágar, two islands west of my destination on Eysturoy. After years of anticipation, my arrival seemed rather anticlimactic. I was a tourist who didn't speak the language, getting my passport stamped, collecting my luggage, going through customs, exchanging dollars for Faroese kroner, and trying to find out how to get to my hotel. I think I was the only one on the plane who didn't speak the language. The airport personnel were very helpful, and they had the bus wait for me while I finished all of my airport business. I was to take a bus that would cross on the ferry to the island of Streymoy, and somewhere in the middle of Streymoy the driver was to help me transfer to another bus that would take me to the island of Eysturoy, where a third bus would take me to the village of Eiði. I paid for a two-week transportation pass without any idea of how much I was actually paying, since I was very tired and wasn't quite sure of the exchange rate.

I stepped outside the door of the small airport into the light rain, and found the bus waiting at the curb. The wind was fresh and cold.

3

I loaded my luggage into the back of the bus and found a seat. The bus ride was a blur of impressions. I didn't want to miss anything. Green, very green hills. Fields of yellow flowers. Creeks that rushed through narrow gorges and then dropped into waterfalls at a cliff's edge. Sheep scattered on the hillsides, long wool trailing to the ground. Small towns and villages near the water along every bay, houses painted brightly. A very well maintained two lane road crossed the island, up and down hills and along the coastline. The road ended abruptly at a dock, and the ferry was coming toward us. Across the water, through the clouds, was another island with green hills, steep cliffs, waterfalls, and more villages.

The bus, several trucks, and a long line of cars were loaded onto the ferry. I followed the other passengers up to the cabin of the ferry and then out to the deck for the short ferry ride. I wanted to see as much as possible of the islands, the birds, the ocean – but I especially wanted to get out of the smoke-filled cabin and into the fresh air. One half of the cabin was non-smoking, but even that side was filled with a gray haze. The wind was even stronger in the sound between the two islands, and it was still raining lightly. As we neared the harbor on the island of Streymoy, I followed the other passengers down the stairs and onto the bus. Ours was the first vehicle off of the ferry, and we were once again on our way up the winding road, crossing the island of Streymoy. I had been travelling for over 24 hours, and I dozed on and off as we traveled through the mist. The bus driver didn't speak English, and he neglected to tell me when to transfer to the next bus, so instead of going to Eysturoy, I remained on the bus and ended up in the capital city of Tórshavn on the southern part of Streymoy.

I collected my luggage and went into the small bus terminal. The clerk understood enough English to let me know that I had a 2½ hour wait for the next bus to Eysturoy. I bought a map of the islands along with a bus and ferry schedule. I wanted to make sure I could see where I was and where I was going.

While waiting at the bus terminal in Tórshavn, I really regretted my tendency to over-pack. Travelling into the unknown I had wanted to be prepared for anything, and I had brought a small carry-on case, a larger suitcase (with wheels), and a very large suitcase (also with wheels).

A JOURNEY INTO THE PAST

This last suitcase had been damaged, and it refused to stand upright, even when propped against a wall. There was no place in the terminal to store them while I explored the city, and dragging them with me was out of the question. It had been difficult enough to get everything into the terminal from the bus.

After all of the other passengers had left the terminal, I put my belongings in the corner and stepped outside the glass doors to look around. The rain had stopped, and the sun shone intermittently through the clouds. I could hear the sound of sea gulls and other birds. The terminal was near a large harbor, and a large ferry was just leaving the dock. There seemed to be a ferry terminal on the upper level above the bus terminal. The harbor was a busy place, and a number of fishing boats, freighters, and small boats were arriving or departing. On one side was a large commercial dock and on the other was a marina with many small boats. I admired a row of impressive looking red buildings just beyond the marina, built right up to the edge of the water on a small, rocky peninsula. Later I learned that these were the historic parliament building, in use for hundreds of years.

Looking in the opposite direction, I could see the city of Tórshavn, spreading up from the harbor and across the rolling hills. It appeared to be a modern, well-maintained city. Nearby I could see hotels, shops, and a residential area. Traffic continuously passed by on the main street near the terminal – cars, trucks, busses, and taxis. By now the airplane snacks from the morning flight were a distant memory. I walked across the parking lot to a nearby kiosk that sold newspapers, magazines, candy bars, and other snacks, where I bought a candy bar and dreamed of a real dinner at my hotel. I didn't see any English language newspapers.

After what seemed like a very long time, the bus for Eysturoy arrived, and my trip continued. With my new map, I followed our progress back up the road I had taken earlier, to the crossroads where I should have changed busses. The road continued to wind along the edge of bays, across green hills, and through an occasional tunnel, stopping at many small towns along the way. At one stop, our bus filled with school children returning from a trip, and their sleeping bags, pillows, and knapsacks filled the back of the bus, completely burying my luggage. Again I dozed intermittently, lulled by the movement of the bus and the sound of rain. The crossing between islands from Streymoy to Eysturoy was very simple – no ferry this time, just a bridge. I watched very carefully for the sign for Oyribakki, where I would change busses again. This third bus would take me north to the town of Eiði and my hotel.

The road followed the edge of the island, and I could see the hills and streams on Streymoy across the narrow sound. Only a handful of people were on this bus, and most of them got off at small villages along the way. Four passengers and the bus driver arrived in

Tinganes, the historic seat of government in the Faroe Islands, sits on a rocky spit of land surrounded by water, with residential Tórshavn in the background.

A JOURNEY INTO THE PAST

Eiði, where we stopped to unload on the main street of the village. Houses were scattered across the hill above us, and far up the hill was a sign for Hotel Eiði. I couldn't imagine how I would get up that hill with all of my suitcases. I spoke to the driver a single word "Hotel?" and pointed up to the sign. He understood immediately, and agreed to drive to the hotel. The narrow winding road was closely lined with houses, and I was sure the standard sized bus would get wedged in place on a sharp curve. At one turn, the front of the bus was just inches from the corner of one house while the back of the bus was just inches from another house on the opposite side of the road. Somehow the bus driver made it through and up to the hotel without damaging anyone's property.

Hotel Eiði was perched on the side of a hill above the town. My room was on the third floor (three trips with suitcases, since I was embarrassed to ask for help), and there was a skylight in the sloped roof. It was 6:00 p.m. when I got to the hotel, and after 29 hours of travel I was grimy and exhausted. I took a shower and went straight to bed, not bothering with the long anticipated dinner. Even though I was tired, I had trouble sleeping, probably because of the 8-hour time difference, anticipation about my visit, and feelings of being in a strange place, so different from any place I had ever been. During the night I was awakened by the sounds of rain pounding on the skylight and strong winds whistling around the hotel, and I got up to watch the storm through the skylight. At midnight the sky was barely getting dark, and then by 1:00 a.m. it was already starting to get light again. By 4:00 a.m. I was wide awake and hungry, but the hotel dining room wouldn't open for several hours. I opened my luggage and took out the packet of my father's letters. They were yellowed with age and brittle, and I handled them carefully. The oldest ones had been written from this island 80 years earlier and had traveled with my father around the world. Even if I couldn't find his family, I hoped I would find someone who would translate them for me. I re-read one of the letters that had already been translated. As on all of the letters, the town of Fuglefjord was written in the upper right hand corner.

☙

THE MISSING SON — A FAROE ISLAND SAGA

Fuglefjord, 18 January, 1923

Dear Brother,

I will write you and let you know how we are. We are well and wish you the same. I want to let you know that I have got a son; his name is Poul Jacob and he is six months old. You have to write soon. Jacob asks if you can buy a harmonica for him, but it is so much to ask of you.

I do not know so much news. Nordlyset sank and all the men died. Three of them were from Fuglefjord, Fredag and 2 young men Martin Georg and Ole Jacob Jacobsen.

Dear brother, are you never thinking about coming home again? Send us a photo so we can see how you look. We hope to hear from you.

Loving regards from us all, children and Johannes.

From your sister,

Malene Hansen

ৎৎ

It was a short letter, but it said so much: the birth of a child, an older child who loved music, the dangers of making a living from the sea, the heartbreak of never again seeing a son or a brother.

Today I planned to visit the town of Fuglafjørður. Poul Jacob Hansen was one of the few names I knew. Was he still alive? Was he still in the Faroe Islands? Was he perhaps still in Fuglafjørður? On a whim I opened the telephone book on the desk. It seemed to be sorted by island. I located the section for Eysturoy. There were many Hansens as well as many Jacobsens. There was even one entry for a Poul Jacob Hansen in Fuglafjørður, followed by a note of "el." but after 75 years, it seemed a remote chance that this was the cousin from the letter. Well, there wasn't much point in my making a phone call, since I didn't speak the language, anyway. Instead, before it got too late, I got down to the practical business of figuring out how to make an international phone call to let my husband know that I had arrived. 7:00 a.m. Faroe time was 11:00 p.m. the previous night in California.

Finally, I went downstairs, hoping to get some breakfast and find out how to get to Fuglafjørður. Breakfast was not quite ready, so I went outside while I waited. The rain had stopped, though the skies were still overcast. Below me was the town of Eiði, with its small white wooden church and the churchyard/cemetery next to it. A breakwater provided protection for a small harbor and marina, and boats were coming and going. To the south were green (very green) hills and cliffs on either side of the narrow sound that separated the two islands. To the north the hill continued above the hotel with wide open space, grass, and rocks. I heard the sounds of birds in the distance. A cold wind was blowing across the hill, fresh from the North Atlantic Ocean, and I was glad for my warm coat, scarf, and thick woolen socks.

I went back into the hotel's warm dining room for breakfast, a buffet of breads, crackers, cheeses, preserves, yogurt, cereals, coffee, tea, and juices. Hans Peter, proprietor and cook, welcomed me in fluent English. I asked him how I could get to the town of Fuglafjørður and explained that I was hoping to find my father's family. He said he had friends in Fuglafjørður and offered to make some phone calls while I ate breakfast. I gave him my list with the little information I had about my father's family, giving the names of my grandparents and my father's brothers and sisters.

By the time I finished eating, Hans Peter had found some information about my cousins – this between his duties of cooking, serving, and talking with all of the hotel guests. Apparently I had some cousins who lived in Fuglafjørður, and he was waiting for a phone call to find out more information. He also explained how I could take a bus or a taxi back to Oyribakki to connect with the main bus route going to Fuglafjørður. Eiði did have a single taxi. Eiði is about 8½ miles from Fuglafjørður in a straight line, but by car it is nearly 25 miles, as the roads primarily skirt the edges of the island.

While waiting for Hans Peter and his telephone research, I took a short walk up the hillside above the hotel. The intermittent rain had changed to a light mist. I was starting to understand why the hills were so green and why every cliff had its waterfall. Around the hill to the east I could see another small bay far below, with the water stretching to meet the overcast skies in the distance. A rectangular patch of bright green grass on the edge of the bay caught my attention. A soccer field! It looked to me as though an errant kick would send the soccer ball into the open ocean on its way to the Arctic Circle. Later someone told me that during games, a boat is ready and waiting to fish balls out of the water. From this hillside view, I could see that Eiði was perched on a narrow isthmus between the headlands where I was standing and the main part of the island to the south. Later I learned that the word "eiði" means isthmus.

The rain returned making the hillside slippery, so I went back to the hotel to find out if Hans Peter had more news for me. He did. Two cousins wanted to come meet me at the hotel at 1:00 p.m. Hans Peter said they were very insistent that he was to keep me at the hotel. They didn't want to miss me or lose track of this cousin from America.

Later I pieced together the story of what had happened that morning after I spoke to Hans Peter. First, he called Sigvør, an old school friend, whose maiden name was Jacobsen. She didn't recognize the names of Joen Magnus and Nikolina Jacobsen (my grandparents), but she did know that Peter Martin Petersen, from the Fuglafjørður Tourist Information Office, was a local historian who would know. Peter Martin was familiar with the story of the young sailor, Hans Jacobsen, who left the islands in the early 1900's and never returned. Just a few days prior to my arrival, he had spent some time with one of the elderly men in the village who was a young child when my father left home. They reminisced about the young Hans Jacobsen, and wondered if he had been lost at sea, or had died in one of the many earthquakes in far off San Francisco, or perhaps had been killed in the war. Peter Martin knew the Jacobsen family, including Malene Hansen's son Poul Jacob, who lived just a few blocks away in Fuglafjørður.

When Hans Peter telephoned Poul Jacob to tell him there was a cousin from America staying at the hotel in Eiði, Poul Jacob replied, "I don't have a cousin from America." Once he was convinced that I was his cousin, he made a series of phone calls that spread the news to relatives all across the islands. When he called his cousin Esmann, the expression of shock on Esmann's face was enough to send his wife, running to pick up an extension phone. Whatever the news was, she wanted to hear it firsthand. When they called their children a short time later, Sigvør wasn't at all surprised. Thinking about her earlier conversation with Hans Peter, she realized that Joen, Magnus, and Nikolina were common family names for her father's family; there were more than a dozen family members – aunts, uncles, cousins – with those names. Perhaps Joen Magnus and Nikolina did fit somewhere in her family tree.

My cousins (what a strange thought in this remote place, "my cousins") arrived right on time. Poul Jacob was the youngest and only living child of Malene Hansen, my father's sister. He was a retired electrician, which explained the abbreviation "el." in the phone book. With him were his wife Jutta, son-in-law Bernhard, and cousin Diana. Diana was the daughter of my father's brother Johannes, and later I would meet her three brothers, Esmann, Martin, and Johannes.

Hans Peter showed us to a private section of the dining room and served us coffee and pastries. With Bernhard acting as interpreter, we spent the afternoon talking, reading old letters, and looking at family photographs I had brought. Bernhard read aloud some of the old letters – some from Poul Jacob's mother Malene, and some from Diana's father Johannes. I still didn't know what the letters said, but now I had relatives who would translate them for me. In addition to the letters from family, there were a few from Thomina, who was raised by my grandparents after her mother died. She was several years younger than my father and was living in a rest home in Fuglafjørður. There was also a stack of letters from Maren, love letters she had written to my father from 1917 to 1923. My cousins had known Maren, and Poul Jacob was a friend of her son, who lived in Denmark. I also showed my cousins photographs of my father, including some he had saved from his early days of sailing.

Poul Jacob and Jutta invited me to stay in their home during my visit, and Bernhard agreed to come back the next day to get me. There wasn't room for me and my luggage in their small car that was already filled with four people. I also thought it would be considerate to give Jutta a chance to prepare for company, though after I got to know her better I realized that she was always prepared.

OVERLEAF:
The Fuglafjørður Bay opens to the narrow sound between the islands
of Eysturoy and Kalsoy, and the snow covered mountains
on three sides of the bay tower over the town of Fuglafjørður. ➤

THE MISSING SON — A FAROE ISLAND SAGA

Fuglafjørður, March 2006: I am living in a place where all the rules have changed, and I am trying to learn the new ones.

- *Accept rides from strangers, especially in the rain. It rains 300 days a year.*
- *Houses don't have doorbells. No one knocks on the door. Whether visiting a relative, a friend, or a stranger, just open the door and go in.*
- *Remember to offer coffee and tea to any visitors, and be sure to have refreshments to serve at a moment's notice. Even if someone comes to the wrong house by mistake, offer coffee and tea.*
- *Don't ask the baby's name until after the christening, often several months after the birth.*
- *Don't expect an invitation to a wedding. Weddings are considered church sacraments, and the service is open to anyone who wishes to attend.*
- *In the winter, the sun rises and sets in the south. In the summer it rises and sets in the north. In summer, night is not dark.*
- *The North Star is almost directly overhead.*
- *The computer keyboard has strange characters on it, and the keys with punctuation marks are all in the wrong places. There is no dollar sign, nor is there an @ sign.*
- *To make long distance phone calls, use the computer.*
- *At home we eat sandwiches with our hands. Here we eat sandwiches with a knife and fork.*
- *At home we eat pancakes for breakfast with a fork. Here we eat pancakes (rolled with sugar) for dessert with our fingers.*
- *At home, if you have a meal of bread, it is probably because you don't have anything else in the house. In novels, bread and water is served to prisoners or naughty children. Here, be sure you never turn down an invitation to a meal of bread. It is a delightful treat. It starts with a piece of dark, dense Scandinavian bread, piled high with different toppings – such as ham, roast beef, fish, or shrimp, with many different garnishes – such as tomato, cucumber, lemon slices, orange slices, pineapple, grated carrots, caviar, each with its own specially seasoned topping – such as mayonnaise or mustard or some other unknown sauce, and all arranged by an artist. Each piece of bread is a colorful work of art that tastes at least as good as it looks. It is almost a pity to ruin the bread by cutting into it with your knife and fork, but it tastes so good it would be a shame not to. This bread is a meal, and it definitely needs a knife and fork.*

Facts about the Faroe Islands

Population: 49,000 people, 80,000 sheep
Population of Tórshavn, the capital city: 18,000
Population of Fuglafjørður, my father's home town: 1600
Temperature range: high 68 degrees F, low 25 degrees F
Location: east of Iceland, west of Norway, north of Scotland, south of the Arctic Circle (62 degrees N, 7 degrees W)
Daylight hours in winter: 5 (less if the clouds are thick)
Daylight hours in summer: 23, plus an hour of twilight
Wind: violent storms have gusts of wind up to 200 mph, a result of winds being funneled between steep cliffs and narrow mountain passes.

Chapter 2 – Fuglafjørður History

Eysturoy is a long narrow island – 23 miles long and 8 miles wide. A number of long narrow bays, or fjords, nearly cut the island in half from end to end. Fuglafjørður is located on a large, deep bay on the eastern side of the island and is surrounded on three sides by mountains 1950 to 2450 feet high. This bay is a natural harbor, well protected from storms of the open ocean by the neighboring islands of Kalsoy and Borðoy. Fuglafjørður has had a fishing and shipping industry since before my father's time. Mount Husafelli is just adjacent to the commercial dock, and large caves have been dug under the mountain and turned into freezers for storing the fish unloaded from trawlers and other commercial fishing vessels. Five freezers are in use, and each one about the size of two or three large gymnasiums. This underground cold storage facility holds 12,000 metric tons of fish and fish products.

Adjacent to the Fuglafjørður harbor is a factory that uses fish and fish products to manufacture fish food pellets used by the many salmon fisheries located throughout the Faroe Islands. When the wind comes from the east, the smell of fish from the factory permeates the whole town, though the residents are used to the smell and it doesn't bother them. It is the smell of prosperity and job security. The salmon fisheries are wire mesh circles, fifty to one hundred feet in diameter, located in the open waters surrounding the islands. The fish food pellets are forced through long hoses from the shore to the fisheries to automatically feed the young salmon around the clock. It takes about three years for the salmon to grow from fingerlings to commercial size. Faroese fisheries supply a large portion of the Atlantic salmon that is sold in stores and restaurants throughout Europe.

Fuglafjørður was one of the earliest settlements in the Faroe Islands. Remains of a Viking settlement from about 950 A.D. were discovered near the sandy beach where the Gjógvará creek enters the bay. There are records from the 13th or 14th century of a man named Rádni oman Lon who lived near this same beach, who rowed his Viking cargo ship to Norway each year to sell and buy goods. My father's family home,

Boats are reflected in the still waters of the Fuglafjørður marina, and ships and fish factories line the quay beyond the break-water.

called *í Lon*, was in this same location, and may have gotten its name from this Viking trader.

At the time of the first census records in the Faroe Islands in 1801, the town had a population of 128 people with 24 houses and a church in three separate small settlements. The population remained fairly steady until the end of the century, when the growth of the fishing and shipping industry in Fuglafjørður brought an increase in the population. In 1901, when my father was 5 years old, the town had a population of 323 people, 50 homes, plus a church, a school, and three businesses. By 1911, there were 445 people, and in 1920 there were 658 people, doubling the population in 20 years.

The first fishing smack with a home port in Fuglafjørður was acquired in 1892. Between 1900 and 1925, many more wind-powered ships were purchased from the British, who were converting to steam powered trawlers. Five small motorboats, manned by 5-6 men, were acquired between 1905 and 1915. Fuglafjørður has a large, deep, well-protected harbor, and during the early 1900's the shipping and fishing industry grew rapidly, and a wooden quay was built on the east side of the bay in 1914. Several factories for salting and drying fish were also established, providing many employment opportunities in the town. Ice houses were filled with snow during the winter and were used to freeze herring to be used as bait by the fishing smacks.

When my father was growing up, the school in Fuglafjørður provided primary education, teaching first through seventh or eighth grades, and my father finished school at age 14 or 15. Public schooling was established in the Faroe Islands in 1872, and a school was built in Fuglafjørður ten years later. A dance hall was built in the early 1900's, and dances for the young people were held there most weekends from September until Lent.

The only volcanic evidence in the Faroe Islands is the warm spring on the southern side of the bay, opposite the town. Since the 13th or 14th century the waters of this spring were thought to have curative powers, which were strongest on the "old" Midsummer, the night between the 3rd and 4th of July, when many people would visit the spring. This has developed into the annual Fuglafjørður Warm Springs (Varmakelda) festival, which includes a midnight bonfire and dance near the spring.

In addition to curing diseases, the warm spring waters also supposedly promote romance and love.

I was able to trace the history of my father's family in Fuglafjørður back several generations. Each home or building in the town had a name, and each census listed the head of each house along with a count of the number of people in each household. During this time, family names were not used, and each child was given a surname that was the father's first name, followed by "son" or "daughter". My father was in the first generation to keep the same surname as his father, but rather than using the surname, people were identified by the house where they were born. My father was known as Hans í Lon.

Here are some of the generations from *í Lon* house:

JAKUP JOHANNESSEN (1717) AND ELSBETH NICHLASDATTER, PARENTS OF

KLEIN JAKUPSEN (1750) MARRIED ANNA AGUSTINIUSDATTER, PARENTS OF

KATRINA KLEINSDATTER (1781)

ISAK JOENSEN MARRIED SUNNEVA NICLASDATTER (1747), PARENTS OF

JOEN ISAKSEN (1770) MARRIED MAREN JACOBSDATTER, PARENTS OF

JACOB JOENSEN (1810) MARRIED SIGGE SOPHIE JOENSDATTER, PARENTS OF

JOEN MAGNUS JACOBSEN (1853) MARRIED NIKOLINA SUSANNA KLEIN, PARENTS OF

HANS NIELS PETER SOPHUS JACOBSEN (1896) – MY FATHER

The í Lon house was typical of many in the village, with a sloped sod roof with a hole at the peak in the center of the house above the stove and fireplace, two small rooms, and a loft for storing food and supplies. Peat was burned for heating and cooking, and lighting was provided by oil lamps. Narrow sleeping cupboards were in the walls around the edge of the rooms and were closed with curtains or doors. There weren't any actual bedrooms.

My son, Jonathan Henke, is sitting in one of the sleeping cupboards under the eaves of the old museum house in Fuglafjørður, just next door to my father's family home.

THE MISSING SON — A FAROE ISLAND SAGA

My grandfather had built an extra room at one end of the house to accommodate his large family. Nine people were listed in í Lon house in the 1901 census. The 1911 census listed eleven people, including my grandparents, four children (Malene, Johannes, Joen, and Hans), their foster daughter Thomine Poulsen, and four other relatives who needed a place to live. Over the years, my grandparents brought up four foster children in addition to their own family.

Three of my father's siblings died before he left home. Sigga Magdalena died at age three in 1896 when my father was an infant. His oldest brother, Jacob Sigvald, died when he fell from the rigging of a ship in 1900 at age 20. Poul Jacob died from tuberculosis in 1916 at age 32.

My father and his two brothers, Johannes and Joen, were all sailors, and each of them began sailing full time as soon as they finished school. Johannes and Joen were both certified as skippers in their early 20's, and they sailed through both world wars, and continued sailing until the late 1940's.

Family ties seem to be very strong in the Faroes. As I met my father's family, I was amazed that for several generations, nearly everyone remained in the Faroe Islands, and the great majority of them remained in their parents' hometown or the hometown of their husband or wife. Out of seventeen cousins, only one left the Faroes to live in Denmark, and of my cousins' children, only two left the Faroes to live in Denmark.

I had some difficulty in tracing my father's family, and my cousin Joen Hansen, son of Malene, was the most confusing. Eventually I learned that the name "Joen" is the Danish spelling for the Faroese name "Jógvan," and in old written records, Joen and Jógvan are often used interchangeably. When Jógvan Hansen was a young man there were several other men in Fuglafjørður with the same name, and my cousin got quite tired of the confusion, so he changed his surname to Kambsdal, after a nearby town. It took me more than a year to discover that Joen Hansen and Jógvan Kambsdal were the same person, the older brother of the Poul Jacob I was staying with.

After Joen and Malene were married in 1917, they lived in í Lon with my grandparents. In 1922-23 they took down the old í Lon house and built a new house, and my grandparents continued to live with them until my grandfather died in 1927 and my grandmother in 1934.

22

FUGLAFJØRÐUR HISTORY

My cousin Ninna remembers her grandparents well, and she told me a little about what life was like during those early years from her own memories and stories she heard from other people. Nikolina Susanna Klein came to Fuglafjørður from the town of Strendur as a young girl, probably to work in a home doing childcare and housework. Eventually she married Joen Magnus í Lon Jacobsen, and they soon had their own family. At that time, there was no school in Fuglafjørður, so Nikolina taught her own children as well as others in the village how to read. She loved music, and she passed this on to her children and grandchildren. One man from the church said that when Nikoline í Lon came to the church, there was always much more life in the hymn singing. Jens Christian Guttesen, orchestra conductor in Tórshavn for many years, recalled living in Fuglafjørður for a year as a young man in about 1918, often visiting the í Lon home. Whenever he was there, the song book would come down from the rafters and the whole family would join in the singing.

Life in Fuglafjørður in the late 1800's and early 1900's was difficult and the work was strenuous, but each person did what they could and worked together. Malene í Lon remembered a time when she was growing up when her father and brothers would take the rowboat to Klaksvík to sell fish. It was difficult to get goods and supplies in Fuglafjørður, and money was hard to come by. The shop in Klaksvík would trade goods for the fish. After they rowed to Klaksvík and docked at the wharf, they discovered that the shop had gone bankrupt and was closed. As a teenager, Malene helped as much as she could by spinning wool and knitting socks, mittens, and sweaters to earn a few kroner. Her brothers would go fishing in the Fuglafjørður bay, and bring home a bucket of good coal fish, and they usually had some salted pilot whale meat in a barrel. When Ninna was young, the family owned sheep and cows, and sometimes they could earn money by selling the sheepskins.

My grandmother (Omma) spun very fine wool, and she taught her granddaughters to knit, beginning with knitting mittens for the sailors. Omma also wove very fine fabric, which she used to make coats for the family. Using the fleeces from the sheep as the raw material, she made all of the clothes for the entire family. She also helped make food for the family, baked the bread, and helped care for the children. Omma and Malene also had to take care of the soaking wet woolen clothes

23

when the men returned from the sea or the children returned from playing on the beach. To dry clothes, they would lay them on the grass and then put stones on them to keep them from blowing away.

Joen made the family's shoes, with thick wooden soles and leather tops from sheepskins or calfskins. The center part of the sheepskin, along the back, was the thickest and strongest part, and that was used for men's shoes. Along the sides, the sheepskin was thinner, and that was used for women's and children's shoes. The best and strongest leather was from the cows, and that was used to make men's boots.

Omma had beautiful white boots that Ninna admired very much. One day when Ninna was about 5 or 6 years old, when no one was looking, she put on Omma's boots and went outside to play. The boots felt so light and comfortable, not like the heavy wooden clogs she usually wore. The next time Omma took her boots out to wear, she discovered that they were covered in mud.

My grandfather (Abbi) was an oarsman for an 8-man boat, which was very strenuous work, but often they couldn't go out because of the weather. He and his sons worked together on the work that had to be done at home. They cultivated grain, potatoes, and turnips, and they made a cultivated field for growing hay for the cows. They carried peat down from the hills near Kambsdal, and sometimes they took the boat to bring peat back from Strendur.

Abbi took care of the sheep all year, in all weather. The sheep grazed in the fields near Kambsdal, and when Anna, Joen's daughter, was about 5 years old, she begged to go with him to the sheep. It was cold and snowing, so they dressed Anna very warmly, and she went with him. There was a ewe with twin lambs that needed to be brought down from the mountain, and Anna carried one of the lambs all the way down the mountain, while Abbi led the ewe and the other lamb. Anna's lamb lived for many years near the í Lon house, and it was called Loni Lamb. Abbi was very proud of little Anna.

There was also time for play. Sometimes Abbi would take the children rowing out on the bay. In the summer the children would play on the beach or slide down the smooth rocks in the Gjógvará creek. The boys would go swimming in the deep pool, but Omma wouldn't let the girls swim, because they must keep their clothes on. In the winter they would slide down the snowy hillsides.

Ninna remembers when the road into Fuglafjørður was completed in 1925. It was built in two sections, from Søldarfjørður to Gøta and from Gøta to Fuglafjørður. When the road was completed, and the first car drove into Fuglafjørður, Omma was amazed and exclaimed, "Jesus have mercy on me."

Abbi and Omma were godfearing people, who led their children and their grandchildren to God's house. Their greatest grief was their fear that their youngest son, Hans, was out in the world leading a sinful life. They spoke about him every day, and when the letters stopped coming after 1924, they feared that he was dead.

As a child, Ninna was sure that the reason her uncle Hans did not return was that his old home had been torn down, and now he would have no place to live.

OVERLEAF: My father's brother Johannes Jacobsen and his wife Mærgretha. ➤

February 2010: *I have been visiting the Faroe Islands off and on for more than thirteen years. I doubt that there is any place else where one can learn the Faroese language.*

My first few visits were for a few weeks at a time during the summer. I knew that I couldn't learn the language during a short visit, but I did try to learn a few every-day, common words. Since many items of food were already labeled, I decided that was a good place to start. There were canisters in the kitchen labeled for flour, sugar, tea, and coffee. There were labels on milk, eggs, butter, marmalade, lunch meat, cheese, and I would try to pronounce these rather strange words.

Years later I learned that most of the words I learned during these early visits were Danish words, since items imported from Denmark logically had Danish labels. Most Faroese people speak Danish fluently. When learning Faroese, it is very important to ask: "What language is that, again?"

Chapter 3 – Letters from the War Years, 1917-1919

When my father was at sea, his brothers and sister wrote to him regularly, and my father saved their letters beginning in 1917. Malene was 14 years older than my father; Johannes, 9 years older, and Joen 6 years older. At the time my father left home in 1916, Malene was married to Johannes Hansen, and they had two children. Johannes Paoli was married to Margretha, and they also had two children. Joen married Malene in 1917, about a year after my father left the Faroe Islands.

World War I was a difficult time in the Faroe Islands, even though they weren't directly involved in the war. It was very dangerous to work in the fishing or shipping industries, and there was always a risk of ships being torpedoed or captured by German and British ships or being destroyed by mines. As a result, there were often shortages of imported products needed for daily life – petroleum, oil, coal, candles, and most foods. Letters from my father's brothers and sister give a picture of some of the difficulties the Faroese people endured during the war.

∽

THE MISSING SON — A FAROE ISLAND SAGA

Fuglefjord, 20 April 1917

Dear Brother,

We have received your letter from 19 March and we are glad to hear from you. We are all well except your sister. She has been in the hospital for 2 months, now she is a little better.

We have not gotten goods from other countries for 2 months, and therefore we have gotten ration cards for bread and sugar, 3½ pounds flour and 1 pound sugar each week, but just now a ship has arrived with food products, therefore we now have enough for 5 months.

The weather in March and April has been very stormy. The ships have not fished the most of this time. The sea has been very rough, so many ships have been damaged. When they can go out, the fishing is very good at Faroe Bank, 250 skippund, but unfortunately many ships cannot go out because they cannot get any salt. The ship Thor *is one of these, and therefore I am at home. Maybe the salt will come in May.*

Joen, your brother, is fishing the south coast of Iceland with the ship Nordlyset. *We have not heard anything from them, but it has also been very stormy there. A telegram has come from Iceland saying that a ship* Beinisvor *has lost a man.*

The last Easter day there was a hurricane. The ship Ruth *was anchored in the harbor in Fuglefjord, and it was blown aground, but it has come out again.*

Write to me as soon as possible. Greetings from your parents. Loving greetings from me.

    Johannes P. Jacobsen

⌒∽

Fishing has always been the mainstay of the Faroese economy, and my father, his brothers, his brother-in-law, and his father were all sailors. Johannes was part owner and skipper of the ship *Thor* from 1916 to 1918. Even today, many of the men that I met in the Faroe Islands were fishermen or sailors at some time. Many of the letters mentioned the size of the catch of fish, using the *skippund* as the unit of measure, equal to 160 kilograms.

The location of the Faroe Islands made them very dependent on the shipping industry for supplies. To the south it is 250 miles to Scotland and 775 miles to London ports. Iceland is 280 miles to the west or 500 miles to the population center of Reykjavik. Norway is 450 miles to the east.

One of the richest fishing areas in the waters around the Faroe Islands is the Faroe Bank, 50 miles southwest of Suðuroy, the southernmost island of the Faroes, where an underwater range of mountains attracts large schools of fish during much of the year.

∽

Fuglefjord, 12 June 1917

Dear Brother,

Yesterday, with great pleasure, we got a letter from you. We were so happy to hear from you. It has been such a long time since we last heard from you, and the times today are so dangerous. Eight ships were sunk on the Faroe Bank and all the men were saved. Mazeppa *has just come from Faroe Bank and had caught 100 skippund in five weeks, and then sailed again. Because it was very calm they were not staying out so long. Mr. Petersen insisted that he sail out with the ship* Erhard *to warn the other ships, and told them what had happened.* Beinir *was one of the ships that were sunk.*

Dear brother, now I will tell you how we are. We are well and wish you the same. I have had a bad winter. I was at the hospital for two months and had an operation. Zachariassen and Herup and a nurse from Torshavn did the operation. I am still a little weak. My dear brother, kind regards from your parents. They thank you for the letter and ask if you have received a letter from them. Mother wishes to know when you may come home again. She asks for a picture of you as a remembrance.

Aliseander came to Fuglefjord the last Pentecost day. Kind regards from your parents and the whole family, first and last from your sister.

Mrs. Malene Hansen

Be well, and write again

∽

Malene Hansen, my father's sister, as a young woman.

The ship *Beinir* was owned by S. P. Petersen, the grandfather of Petur Martin Petersen who had helped me find my relatives in Fuglafjørður. From Petur Martin I learned that, before sinking the ships, the German sailors gave the fishermen a chance to escape in life boats, supplied them with drinking water, and gave them the compass bearings for the nearest land. When news of the lost ships reached Fuglafjørður, the Petersen's used their small motorboats to sail out to the ships fishing in the Northern Seas and warn them not to sail to the Faroe Bank. Johannes was sailing with *Thor* during the last of May 1917, when they saw a motorboat sailing toward them. It was one of the Petersen's boats, coming to tell them about the attack on the Faroese fishing ships.

LETTERS FROM THE WAR YEARS, 1917-1919

Fuglefjord, 20 August 1917

Dear Brother,

We are well, and wish you the same. I bring greetings from your mother, who is ill. Two days ago the doctor was with her, and he said that it was neuritis in the hip and down the legs. My dear brother, you know how much she is longing to see you. She is asking if you will come home again soon. Now it has been 8 days since Thor was here and Petersen bought the fish. I think they have fished 2020 skippund in the past 14 days. Nordlyset has come from Iceland with 200 skippund for 2 months.

Dear brother, times are bad here today. There are no supplies. I hope that God will bring better times for us. In the western part of the Faroes there are plenty of pilot whales. 145 pilot whales were killed in Sorvag. Another pod of whales was also there, but they did not kill them. I saw in the newspaper that the mail would go to Bergen last Sunday, so it will be a long time until you receive this letter.

Kind regards from your parents and the family. Loving greetings from your sister.

Malene Hansen

Write again.

I am sending you here the vaccination certificate.

❦

Included in the papers my father saved was a smallpox vaccination certificate from 1897 when he was one year old, undoubtedly the certificate that Malene sent him.

Whaling is an important part of Faroese life. When a pod of pilot whales is sighted, all boats in the area help drive them into the nearest harbor, where everyone joins in the whale kill. Each town has an official whose job it is to mark the whales into family sized portions. Everyone who participates in the whale kill gets a double portion of the whale meat. Next, everyone in the town gets a portion. Depending on the size of the catch, people from neighboring villages or even neighboring islands can come get their share. A catch of 145 whales (each 9 to 18 feet in length) was enough to be shared with other villages, and undoubtedly helped them survive the times when food and

33

THE MISSING SON — A FAROE ISLAND SAGA

supplies could not be brought in from mainland Europe. Every part of the whale was used. During my father's days, the rendered oil was used in oil lamps and to waterproof the outside walls of their homes. The meat was dried or salted. Even the bones and teeth were used to make tools or jewelry. I have never seen a whale kill, though I have often eaten whale meat – fresh, salted, and dried. I have several pieces of jewelry made from pilot whale teeth. During one of my visits to the Faroe Islands, there was a pilot whale kill of about 75 whales on an island to the east of Eysturoy. A friend of Poul Jacob's gave him some whale meat, which he cut it into small pieces and layered with coarse salt in a small barrel to preserve it. It would take about 4 months to cure. Another time I drove past the nearby Gøta bay just after a whale kill when the bay was red with blood. In these isolated islands where there are few sources of food other than the sea, in order to survive, people take advantage of the food that comes near their shores.

∽

Fuglefjord, 29 October 1917

Dear Brother,

I will now write some words to you and tell you that we are all well. The ships have had good fishing this summer. I was out fishing, but we could not go out before May 15 because the salt had not come to the Faroes, and we stopped fishing in August because the men would not sail to Iceland. They were afraid that they would be taken by English war ships. Thank God all the ships came home again, and they had very good fishing, but there were many ships that were not out fishing. We fished 240 skippund in 3 months.

It is possible that the ships cannot go out fishing next year. We cannot get the things necessary for the ship and the salt is very expensive, 35 kroner a barrel. Thank God we have the things most necessary to live. We cannot buy oil, and therefore we use drawn oil for the lamps.

The weather has been very bad, windy and rainy. The haymaking failed, and therefore we had to kill many cows in the village.

I will send this letter with the ship Beskytteren which is sailing directly to Norway. Edward Hansen will sail with this ship to go to Copenhagen, Denmark, to the doctor. Elin Sofie will take this letter and bring it to you.

Don't forget to write back as soon as you know something. A little message from your dear brother.

J. P. Jacobsen

Your parents, your sister and brother and my wife wish you all the best. Good-bye.

꩜

During the spring of 1917, five ships were sailing from the Mediterranean to the Faroes with a cargo of salt. Four of them were torpedoed near Kirkwall, England, and only one of them made it safely to the Faroes. When fishing ships are out at sea for weeks at a time, it is important to preserve the fish immediately, and my father's brothers couldn't go fishing without salt. Modern fishing ships often have a sophisticated fish processing and freezing plant on board, and I met one young woman (a great grand-daughter of Johannes) who worked one summer in the fish processing and freezing plant on her father's ship.

What a dismal picture this letter gives – danger at sea from war ships, no salt and without salt no chance to earn a living, and a failed hay crop resulting in slaughtering the cows and no milk or cheese. During the war, fishing and other commercial vessels were in danger from both German and English war ships, and this had a severe impact on an economy that relied almost entirely on fishing to bring in income. Very few crops, other than hay, grew successfully in the Faroe Islands, and it was a terrible blow when even the haymaking failed. During the long winter months when skies are dark for 19 hours a day, oil for lamps was a necessity, and the drawn oil from whales was quite inferior to imported oil and provided only a dim smoky light.

꩜

Fuglefjord, 1 April 1918

Dear Brother,

Thank you for the letter I got from you. You cannot believe how glad the children were for the post cards you sent to them. They have just gotten them today, and they thank you for the cards. Greetings from my husband.

He runs a boat for S. P. Petersen; since Christmas he has fished very well. Since Christmas he has made 1200 kroner. For the last while it has been bad weather and no fishing. I don't have any more time now. Let us know when you are coming home again, my dear brother.

Kind regards from all in our house, but first and last from your sister.

Malene Hansen

Write to me again.

∾

The currency used in the Faroe Islands in the early 1900's was the Danish crown. Today the Faroese government has its own paper money, based on the Danish crown, but the people use Danish coins.

During the years from 1917 to 1919 my father sailed with several different ships. Correspondence by mail was not reliable, especially during the war years, and some letters were lost or returned to sender. My grandparents lived with Joen and Malene, and when they wrote to my father, they would dictate the letter to Malene, who would write for them. The first part of this next letter is from the parents, and then Malene completes the letter herself.

∾

Fuglefjord, 1 April 1918

Dear Son,

Today we got a letter from you. Therefore I will not neglect to write again. You have to believe that we have written several letters, but they were not delivered.

My dear son, we are tolerably well, and wish you good health. There has been a little girl born since you sailed, a daughter to Joen your brother. She is a nice little girl. Her name is Anna Dagny. You did not get the letter that was written after they were married.

Dear brother-in-law, I was so glad when I got a letter from you, but when we looked more closely, we saw that it was a letter from me to you that was sent back. It was addressed to the ship Volunteer.

LETTERS FROM THE WAR YEARS, 1917-1919

There have been many changes since you were here, but I hope that you will come home again, and I hope that you will be happy even if we live here for the first time. And maybe we will have gotten a new home when you come. Your parents wish that you will come home again soon. They long with their whole heart to see you again.

You should see our little Anne. She is waving her hands to her uncle while I am writing. She is only ½ year old. My dear brother-in-law, there has never been so many fish in the Faroes before this year. The small boats have fished 100 kroner a day. Your brother Joen has been out fishing 5 tours, and he has gotten about 300 kroner, even though he was only the second master. Now he is with Nordlyset, and you cannot believe how afraid we have been because it has been so stormy and snowing, and we have heard from all of the ships but not from them. We hope for the best, and that God will soon send them back to us. Jacob Martin is with a ship from Vestmanna. Now he is in Vestmanna and he telephoned me yesterday. Hannes is with a Norwegian boat in Iceland for fishing. They should only be out for 14 days. The boat's name is Brian.

Come back to us. You cannot believe how much we all wish you back. You should know that we often talk about you. Your sweetheart often visits me, because she knows that we can talk to each other. She has just been here and sewed something for Easter. My dear Hans, you must not be offended at me for writing this. Write back to me as soon as you can, and send me a photograph of you, and I can show your parents.

I send loving greetings from your parents and sister-in-law.

Malene Jacobsen

I think Nordlyset is coming now. Good-bye. Write again soon.

❧

It is clear from the letters that Malene knew my father well, and she was also a good friend of Maren, my father's sweetheart.

Three letters from my father to his parents have survived, and some of my relatives gave me copies of them. This one was written two years after he left home.

❧

Honningsvaag (Norway), 19 September 1918

Dear Parents,

I will now write you some words and let you know that I am well and wish you the same. I am still with the same boat and we have sailed three times to England. The first time to London, the second time to Hull, and the third time to Blyth, and we shall sail from here tomorrow. Here in the north it is very cold, and in the winter there is light for only one hour a day.

We shall sail from here to Trondheim and from there to England. I do not know when I will come home again. Maybe it will not be so long. This time I do not know any more to write, but I shall write again soon. The last letter I got from home came with Elin Sofie, and now I have to stop this time.

Kind regards,

Hans Jacobsen

Greetings to my sister and brothers.

༄

Honningsvaag is at the northernmost tip of Norway, above the Arctic Circle. The letter from home delivered by Ellen Sofie Petersen was one from Johannes dated 29 October 1917, eleven months earlier. With my father constantly on the move, it took a very long time for letters to catch up to him. From June to September 1918 he was with a British ship called *Southwood*, sailing primarily between England and Norway.

༄

Fuglefjord, 20 July 1919

Dear Brother-in-law,

Thank you for the letter I got from you. It was nice of you to write to me. Now I will tell you how it is at home. We are all well except your parents. They are weak. Your mother is always feeling bad. They were very glad to hear from you, but when they heard what you were writing to me, that maybe you will stay off in America, they were very upset that you are not thinking about coming home again. I tried to comfort them, and said to them that you will come sooner or later.

Your brother Joen is in Iceland with Nordlyset, *and your brother Johannes is at home this summer. He has sold his boat* Thor, *and now he is not the captain any more. They now have three children, and we have one, a little girl. You cannot believe how nice she is. All are so kind to her, especially your father. Every morning he comes into our sleeping room and he takes her in his arms when she looks at him. He is spoiling her. Her name is Anna Dagny.*

I do not know more to write this time, but I hope to hear from you soon. Just before I got the letter I was about to send a telegram and ask if you were alive or not. I am stopping now, and I hope you write again soon.

With kind regards from us all at home, parents, brother, and sister-in-law.

Malene Jacobsen

&

When I first read this letter, I was surprised to read that as early as 1919 my father was talking about moving permanently to America. From my father's sailing records, apparently he made his first trip to the west coast of the Americas in May 1919 with a Norwegian ship, the S/S Otta. In the many years' correspondence, this was the only time there was any mention of him staying in America.

OVERLEAF: Klaksvík on the island of Borðoy is the second largest city in the Faroe Islands. ➤

Klaksvík, June 2008: At about 11:30 p.m. on a Saturday night, I was in a strange city standing in the rain in a parking lot behind a temporary platform waiting for the brass band (called a "horn orchestra") to pack up their instruments to make room on the stage for the choir. Our choir sang in a language that I don't quite understand and that is pretty much unpronounceable for an American tongue. We started with a centuries old ballad about brave Norse men sailing from their homeland over the salty sea, enduring many dangers. We sang about being homesick for the green days of spring, about fishing along the beach in summer, about the green hillsides and the blue fjords, and we sang a song of praise to God. During our thirty minute concert, the rain and wind increased and so did the crowd. By the time we were done, our music was soaking wet and there were about 200 people standing in the rain – people of all ages, from babies in prams and little children running around, to their parents and grandparents.

This was one of those times that I asked myself, "What am I doing here, and how in the world did I get here?"

The short answer is that I drove in my rented car from my rented house in Fuglafjørður, over the pass near Kambsdalur, through the tunnel to Leirvík, then through the long tunnel that goes down, down, down, under the ocean sound, and down a little more, and then up, up, up, passing under a mountain range, and up a little more to the city of Klaksvík, on the neighboring island.

The real answer is a little more complicated. Eleven years ago, this month, I made my first visit to these islands, the Faroe Islands, far, far north in the Atlantic, to the place where my father was born. From the first, I was fascinated by the islands, the scenery, the people, and the culture. And I keep coming back. Over time, the fascination has grown to a love of this place and these people. This visit is my ninth trip in eleven years, but don't you think that the time I stayed for thirteen months should count for more than one visit?

Now, whenever I visit the Faroes, I sing with the choir, or sometimes with two choirs. We were invited to sing for the Klaksvík festival, and that is how I came to be singing in the rain in a foreign language in the middle of the night in a strange city on an island far north in the Atlantic Ocean.

Chapter 4 – Welcome

Planning my trip to the Faroe Islands, I wanted to be prepared for anything. I hoped to find my father's family, but I also came prepared to spend the two weeks by myself. From the first hours in the islands I knew I would enjoy the spectacular scenery, and I had lots of film for my camera. I also brought books to read, including 1463 pages of the unabridged *"Les Miserables,"* in case I had lots of time on my hands.

But I wasn't prepared for what actually happened. The welcome I was given was overwhelming. From the first moment, I was received with open arms, like a long lost child. I was made a part of the family, and a very large family, at that. Eight of my cousins still lived in the Faroe Islands, and I met all of them and many of their families. My cousins were in their 70's and 80's, and many of them had children my age. My father was the youngest child in his family, and he was 45 when he married my mother, so I was quite a bit younger than my cousins.

The feeling of being welcomed started while I was at the hotel, with the kindness of Hans Peter, who went out of his way to help find my family. Poul Jacob and Jutta opened their home to me. They and their family provided meals for me and the many other relatives who stopped by to meet me, and they drove me around the islands for many hours of sightseeing.

43

Back at the Hotel Eiði after my cousins left, I went up to my room and took a long nap. After a very long airline flight and with the eight hour time difference, my jet-lagged body had no idea whether this was day or night, and since it didn't get dark at night, it took me quite a while to keep my days and nights straight. Then I went down to the restaurant for a late dinner, a wonderful meal. During dinner, I was rather surprised when Hans Peter came to tell me I had a phone call, since hardly anyone knew where I was. He led me back into the kitchen to use his phone.

The call was from a relative who wanted to meet me while I was in the Faroes. Anna Katrin had just sailed the Caribbean and Pacific Oceans, from Puerto Rico to Tahiti, and after her return she visited her father, my cousin Hanni. He knew that these were the same waters where his Uncle Hans had sailed 80 years earlier, and they were talking about this uncle when they received a phone call telling them that his daughter was visiting the Faroe Islands. She called to invite me to visit her in her home on the island of Sandoy. I took her phone number and promised to make plans for a visit.

After dinner I sat at my table by the window and tried to sketch the scene of the town, the small harbor, with green hills surrounding it all and fading to purple in the distance. The colors were continually changing in the evening light, and with my small box of colored pencils I couldn't come close to capturing the colors of the hills, cliffs, water, and sky. At 11:00 when I went up to my room the skies were just darkening to dusk. That was the only evening that I spent alone during my two week stay in the Faroe Islands.

Friday morning, Poul Jacob, Bernhard, and Bernhard's 7 year old son Pól Jakku came to the hotel to take me to Fuglafjørður. Pól Jakku was named for his grandfather, but they had used the Faroese spelling instead of the Danish. Bernhard and Lillian had adopted Pól Jakku from the Philippines 5 years earlier when he was 2 years old.

Poul Jacob's house was just a short block up the hill from the main street and the waterfront. The lower level had a small shop selling light fixtures, candles, and gift items. The main part of the house was on the second level, and I moved my luggage into the spare bedroom upstairs. Then I met the rest of the family. Hannis was an electrician, and he lived in his parents' home in rooms on the lower level.

Lillian was just getting ready to start a new job at the local kindergarten, a publicly subsidized preschool for children from age 2 to 6. Her husband Bernhard was working as a house painter, though he had spent years as a sailor and fisherman. On rainy days when he couldn't paint, he and Lillian were often my tour guides and interpreters. Pól Jakku had just finished his first year of school. He was an active, independent boy, and in the summer he spent a lot of time outside, playing with friends and relatives. When his parents went out, they would leave a phone number on the table for him to call them when he came home. As with many children in the Faroes, he had grandparents, aunts, and uncles from both sides of the family living in town, and everyone helped look out for the children.

Gurið (pronounced GOOrih) was Poul Jacob and Jutta's adopted daughter. Her mother, Jutta's niece, died when Gurið was a very small child. Her father was a sailor and fisherman and was unable to care for a small child, so Gurið was raised by her great aunt. Gurið still keeps in touch with her father and three older sisters, who live in Tórshavn. She and Dan had a three year old daughter Heidi and another child on the way. Heidi was very shy around strangers, and she would quickly turn away if she saw me with my camera. I took many photos of the back of her head. Dan worked as a mechanic at one of the fish processing plants in Fuglafjørður, and during the very busy summers when other employees were on holiday, he worked twelve hour shifts six days a week.

These were the people who took me into their homes and their lives and took care of me for the next two weeks. They quickly became my family.

My primary impression of the next few days was of meeting many, many relatives and of eating many meals from fine china dishes in many different homes. Only a few of the older generation spoke English, but most of the people in their 40's or younger had studied English in school, and many of them were quite fluent, so most of the time, there was someone to translate for me. I also took several sightseeing trips around Eysturoy and walked around Fuglafjørður to see what my father's home town was like. In addition to these new experiences, I was also trying to understand a new culture with different customs, but for this, I was on my own. There was no one to explain culture or customs for me, since no one knew the American culture that I was comparing it to. I was hoping that I didn't make too many social blunders or offend my new family.

Meeting so many people in such a short time was overwhelming. Many Faroese names sound very unusual to American ears, and often they were impossible for me to pronounce. Since I wanted to learn who everyone was and how we were related, I tried to write the names in my notebook, but that was difficult, since the Faroese alphabet has a different set of letters than the American one. Next, I decided to ask people to write their own names in my notebook, but that wasn't any better, because I couldn't read what they had written. The script used in writing Faroese is somewhat different from the script we use in America, and often I couldn't figure out what the letters were. I was delighted to meet Dan and Sam, since they were the only two people whose names sounded just the same as American names.

I also found the family relationships complicated. I had brought with me the names of my father's six brothers and sisters, and I discovered that only three of them had survived to have children – Malena, Johannes, and Joen. Eight of my first cousins were still living in the Faroes, and many of the people I was meeting were my cousins' children, grandchildren, or great-grandchildren. As could be expected, the language barrier added to the confusion, such as the time a relative wrote the names of his brothers and sisters when I asked the names of his children.

Friday lunch was the first meal that I ate with the family, and I could see immediately that meal times were different in the Faroes. Jutta served several different kinds of breads and crackers and put a lot of different ingredients on the table, and each person at the table chose the items they wanted for their own sandwiches. Sandwich ingredients included foods that we wouldn't think to serve on bread in America, such as fruit salad mixed with whipped cream, or pickled red cabbage. I had never seen anyone eat a sandwich with a fork and knife, and I had certainly never tried it, myself. I tried eating the Faroese way, with

WELCOME

fork in my left hand and knife in my right, but I felt very awkward. Finally young Pól Jakku asked me why I was holding my fork in such a funny way. I explained that our customs in America were different, and I was trying to copy everyone else and eat the way they do in the Faroes. He gave me a lesson on the proper way to hold my silverware, with my fork in my left hand with the tines pointing down and the knife in my right hand.

Other mealtime customs are different in the Faroe Islands, as well. Very seldom were serving dishes passed around the table, and it is quite acceptable to reach across the table for something, or even to stand up to reach it or to walk around the table to get it. I had the impression that it wasn't polite to interrupt someone to ask them to pass a serving dish, and it was better to find a way to reach the dish yourself. I decided that I should always try to sit near the center of the table where I had a better chance of reaching the food I wanted.

On Friday I met more new people. Marjun and Jóhan Heri Joensen, Poul Jacob's niece and her husband, joined us for lunch. Marjun had a yarn and fabric shop on the main street and Johan Heri taught at the high school. He spoke English fluently and often helped as my translator.

It was a warm, sunny day, so after lunch I took a walk around the neighborhood with Poul Jacob and Diana. In a small town, word had traveled fast, and a lot of people knew who I was and wanted to say hello. I met more relatives and neighbors, including the wife of Poul Jacob's nephew, a grandson of Johannes, and Peter Martin from the tourist office, who had helped me find my family. There were others who stopped us to say hello, though I wasn't always sure whom I was meeting.

We walked through the cemetery, where I visited the graves of my grandparents, aunts, uncles, and cousins. We went out to the marina, where several dozen boats were moored, and from this vantage point I had a good view of the town spread out around us on three sides. I was surprised by how colorful everything was – green hills, blue sky, white clouds, and houses and boats of every color imaginable. This was not at all like a typical suburban housing development in America, where the houses are nearly identical. Then we returned to Poul Jacob's house. This short walk of 8 or 10 blocks had taken us a couple of hours; and rather than seeing much of the town, I had met relatives and friends, instead. It was clear that I was going to be meeting many more, because the family was planning a reunion for Sunday night at a local restaurant.

After dinner, more relatives arrived to meet me – Esmann, son of my father's brother Johannes, and his wife Gunnleyg. I was surprised to find that visitors would come to visit late in the evening. It soon became clear that in the Faroe Islands, a good hostess puts on the coffee pot and sets out refreshments for guests, no matter when they arrive.

Saturday was another warm and sunny day, and after breakfast I went for a walk by myself. I didn't realize yet that it was rare to have warm and sunny days in the Faroes. A creek entered a culvert just across the street, and I followed it up the hill. It was lined with small bushes of yellow daisies with large, rounded petals. I came to the edge of the town after a few blocks, and I continued following the creek up the grassy hillside above the town, soon coming to a concrete sheepfold. Clumps of dirty wool were lying on the ground, and some of it was very long, six or eight inches, in a variety of colors - white, gray, brown, and black.

I sat on a rock beside the creek and took in the scene around me. The wildflowers scattered across the grassy slope were similar to the wildflowers in the hills where I grew up near San Francisco. The lower part of the hillside was divided into large rectangles with barbed wire fences. I could hear the bleating of the sheep grazing in the distance and the call of birds circling overhead and flitting from bush to bush. The distinctive sound of sea gulls is the same on the California coastline as it is here in the North Atlantic. The path followed the creek up the hillside to a pass between two mountain peaks above me, but I was content to sit beside the sheepfold. I pulled out my small notebook to write down my experiences of the past day. Boats moved in and out of the harbor breakwater while I sat on a rock in the warm sun.

The small, isolated town of Funningur is on the edge of Funningsfjørður bay on the north-eastern part of Eysturoy.

    That evening all of Poul Jacob's family came for dinner, and afterwards Poul Jacob and Bernhard took me sightseeing to the northern part of the island. I wasn't used to long daylight hours that would let us start a sightseeing trip at 8:00 or 9:00 in the evening. The road wound through the green hillsides and fields of bright yellow wildflowers. We passed small villages along the water in secluded bays, with high mountain peaks above us. The scenery was breathtaking. We drove through a high valley in the middle of the island, then along winding mountain roads, and suddenly we had a view of a large bay surrounded by mountains on three sides and a small town with brightly painted houses far below us. Bernhard stopped the car often so I could take pictures. At first I was concerned when he would just stop in the middle of the road, but I soon realized that it wasn't a problem, since there was very little traffic.

We drove to the small town of Gjógv (JAEGV) where a deep gorge served as a natural harbor. The sheer rock walls were covered with ferns and wild flowers where water from the hillsides was constantly dripping, and birds were nesting along the upper sections of the cliffs. A fisherman pulled his small boat out of the water onto the rock shelf at the bottom of the gorge, and I could see that fish filled the bottom of his boat. The sea gulls quickly arrived to feast on a meal of fish heads and guts.

Sunday, June 29, was just my fourth day in the Faroe Islands. Each day was filled with so many new experiences, that it seemed as though I had been here much longer. Sunday, by itself, seemed to last a week, and all day long from morning to night I met countless relatives. By night, the cousins I had met earlier in the day seemed like old friends.

Sunday morning I went to church with Poul Jacob and his family. A Lay Reader led the service, since the priest was at one of the other five churches for which he was responsible. The congregational singing was full and rich, and everyone seemed to love to sing. Once the music was over, I had trouble staying awake. The church was warm, I couldn't understand a word that anyone said, and I still felt like I was in the wrong time zone. One wall of the church had windows facing the bay and the town, but even this view didn't keep me awake. I dozed, but we were sitting near the back and at least I didn't slide off of the pew.

After church, we visited Jóhan Heri and Marjun, Poul Jacob's niece and her husband. Jóhan Heri had borrowed my father's letters and papers to prepare a short presentation for the family reunion planned for later that evening. On the wall of their living room was a framed photograph of my father, an enlargement of a photo my father had sent to his family – the same photo that I had brought with me. My father's sister Malene, Marjun's grandmother, had made the enlargement. I also met a number of other family members who stopped to visit.

Next we drove to Gøta for Sunday dinner with Esmann and Gunnleyg and their children and grandchildren. They lived in the home that

The natural gorge at Gjógv, near the northern tip of Eysturoy, serves as a protected harbor.

THE MISSING SON — A FAROE ISLAND SAGA

had belonged to her parents, and they had added a large dining room next to the kitchen, with a wall of windows looking out on their garden. Their home is always open, and they often have crowds of family and friends for meals. Once again, I felt like I was being welcomed into a large, loving family. There were fifteen or twenty of us there for Sunday dinner, though the children soon left to go fishing, and several men left for a soccer game. I thought it might be fun to watch the soccer game, but I seemed to be the guest of honor, so I stayed.

Usually when a large group of people were together for dinner, I noticed that the hostess or her daughter didn't join us at the table, but spent the whole mealtime refilling serving plates, filling glasses, and making sure everyone at the table had everything they needed. When the meal was nearly over, and the children left to play, then the hostess would fill a plate and sit down at the table to eat. This custom was hard to get used to, and it is just about the opposite of good table manners in America. Since I was a small child, I had been taught that at the table, no one should start eating until the hostess sits down and begins eating. On a later visit to the Faroe Islands, my children and I prepared and served a meal for some relatives, and since we didn't have enough chairs, my daughter Natasha insisted that she would be the hostess without a chair.

After dinner, I pulled out my packet of letters and photos from my father, and Esmann's daughter read some of the letters aloud for everyone. Gunnleyg asked me if I would like to talk to a radio broadcaster and tell him my story. An announcer from the radio station was home for Sunday dinner with his mother, who lived nearby, and Gunnleyg invited him to come and talk to me. He was very interested in my story, and invited me to the studio in Tórshavn for an interview.

Sunday evening we walked down to the Muntra, the only restaurant in Fuglafjørður, for a family reunion party. I wasn't at all sure what to expect, but that seemed to be a permanent state of mind for me since my arrival. The family had reserved a large room on the upper floor, with windows overlooking the bay. Bernhard stayed by me most of the evening, translating for me and telling me what to do. We were among the first people to arrive, and Bernhard suggested that I stand near the doorway to greet everyone as they came in. I gave myself a

52

simple goal of repeating each person's name, but it wasn't so simple after all. The Faroese language has endless nuances of vowel sounds that are very unusual for Americans, and sometimes it would take a dozen tries or more to even come close to pronouncing the name right, while those around me laughed and cheered me on. Of course there were the familiar faces of those I had already met. Altogether 65 people showed up, coming from all over the islands.

First, we were served refreshments – coffee, cookies, and a fruit bowl of whipped cream, a variety of fruits, and shaved chocolate. Bernhard then told a little about me and my coming to the Faroes. Jóhan Heri showed some of my father's photos and read several of the letters from my father's brothers and sister – the parents, grandparents, or great grandparents of most of the people in the room. The evening included a lot of music, and many of my relatives were talented musicians. By each place setting there was a booklet of songs, and during the evening everyone joined in singing together. This was a family that loved music. There was also special music by several different family members. Bernhard told me that a relative was going to play the harmonica, but instead what he played was the accordion, and he played with such joy and exuberance that soon everyone was tapping their feet to the music. That was the moment that I realized that in the letters from Malene, her young son wanted an accordion, not a harmonica. (The Faroese word for accordion is "harmonika.")

Eight of my cousins were at the party, as well as the widows of two other cousins: Malene's son Poul Jacob, Petra (widow of Jacob) and Hansina (widow of Jógvan); Johannes's children Esmann, Hanni, Diana, and Martin; and Joen's children Nikoline, Petra, and Aksel. Only two cousins were not at the party; Joen's daughter Magda in Denmark, and my brother Peter in California.

By about 11:30 people started to leave for home, and Bernhard suggested that I stand at the door again to bid everyone farewell. By this time they all felt like old friends. I wasn't exactly sure who everyone was, and I didn't understand any of their language, but I knew I was thoroughly welcomed and loved by my family in the Faroe Islands.

OVERLEAF: My father's brother Joen, his wife Malene, and daughters Nikoline and Anna. ➤

5

Fuglafjørður, June 2008: During the years that I have been visiting the Faroe Islands, I have taken thousands of photos of the spectacular scenery. Many of my favorite photos are on my website, jenniferhenke.com. There are some things that I would like to show you about the Faroe Islands, but I haven't been able to take a picture of them that really does them justice.

- *Storms when the wind blows the waterfalls up hill, rather than down.*

- *It is a still, foggy summer night when everything is quiet and sounds are muffled, and then the silence is interrupted by birds on the steep hillsides arguing over the best places to sleep for an hour or two.*

- *While walking along a deserted road late at night, when people, animals, and birds all seem to be asleep, a startled bird flies up, nearly in my face, from its nest in a ditch beside the road.*

- *Same road, same night, everything silent and muffled, and I pass a hay shed in the shadows beside the road and surprise a grazing pony, who neighs loudly in my ears – BWAAAH HAAAH HAAAH Haaah bwaaah haaah haaa....*

- *I open my window late at night to take a picture of the night sky or the mountains or the ships, and the only sound I hear is the surf on the other side of my fence swishing back and forth in the seaweed.*

- *Several dozen birds are flying in the sky over my head, dipping, diving, swooping, and squawking, trying to scare me away from their nesting grounds.*

Chapter 5 – Letters, 1920-1924

My father's family continued to write to him regularly for several more years. At first, the letters were full of news about family, the economy, or the town, but as time passed, many of the letters were shorter, and more awkward, almost as though they were written to a stranger. I also suspect that, as time passed, it became more and more difficult for my father to write in Danish, since this was not his native language and he seldom had the opportunity to use it. Writing did not come easily for him. He always used a fountain pen with a broad tip, like a calligraphy pen, and he wrote in an old-fashioned formal script, very much like writing in calligraphy. It must have taken him a long time to write a letter to his family.

௸

Fuglefjord 20 January 1920

Dear Brother,

One thing I must tell you about is that I have gotten a daughter. She was born 29 December, and her name is Nikoline Mathilde. She was baptized on 1 January. We now have 2 daughters.

The fishing the last three years has been very good, especially 1919. The ships fished up to 1500 skippund with a value of 180,000 kroner. I was with Nordlyset *last year. We fished 710 skippund, and I got 2600,50 kroner. There have been 25 new ships coming to the Faroe Islands. It has been a bad winter, stormy and snowy, so the fishing has not been good this winter. The British trawlers are in the Faroes again, and therefore we can think that it will not be good for fishing in the coming time. Jacob Martin is going to school this winter to learn to be a captain.*

Brothers and sisters and parents are all well, and wife and children too, and they send you best wishes.

> *Joen F. Jacobsen*

❧

I got to know Joen and Malene's daughter Nikoline on my first trip to the Faroe Islands, and I have often visited her in her home in the capital city of Tórshavn. Her two sons, Henry and Símun, are just the same ages as my brother Peter and me.

Jacob Martin was my father's cousin and was one year younger than him. His mother died when he was a small child, and he lived with my father's family in *í Lon* house when he was young.

❧

Fuglefjord 1 April 1920

Dear Brother,

We were glad to hear from you. I thank you many times for the letter. The children were very glad for the lovely cards you sent to them. There has been bad weather, but it seems that it will now be better. Yesterday it was very foggy with a little rain. Today it is very lovely weather. The sun is shining, no clouds in the sky, and it is as warm as in June. The ship will now sail for the first trip, because the weather has been very bad.

Loving greetings from the children. Joen asks if you are married because you have left us for so long a time. Jacob asks if you can buy him an accordion - he is so glad for song and music. I tell him that he has to wait for better times, and it will be cheaper. To buy him an expensive accordion is maybe not a good idea, but he is so impatient. Johannes sends you kind regards. He is skipper of the boat Erhard. *He has been out fishing 5 tours and he has gotten 800 kroner. I hope to hear from you again soon.*

Kind regards from your sister,
Malene Hansen

∾

This was the first letter that mentioned that Jacob wanted an accordion. I agree with Malene that it would be extravagant to send an accordion half way around the world for an eleven year old boy who wanted to make music. I know that my father loved music, and he played the saxophone and the mandolin.

∾

Fuglefjord, 2 April 1920

Dear Brother-in-law,

Your brother asked me to write for him. He had to leave for fishing the day after he got the letter from you. You cannot believe how glad we are to get a letter from you. It is a very long time between the letters.

The weather has been very bad. No fishing this winter. The ships started this year in March. Your brother is on board Nordlyset. He is the second master. Last year they had made two tours before Easter. This year they did not make any. They will not come back before Easter. If the weather is good I think it will be a long trip.

Greetings from your parents. Every time when we get a letter from you, they ask if you are writing when you will come home again. They are longing very much to see you. Now they are very weak. Your father is often sick.

It is not so easy for me to write because Anna is disturbing me. Anna is now so big that she can play on the beach alone when the weather is good. When you left we were not yet married, and now we have two big girls. Maybe you are waiting to come home until we have gotten a new house. Your father and mother live with us, and when you come, there is also room for you. Now they are building 7 new houses in the village.

With kind regards from us all in this house, your parents, brother, sister-in-law and our children.

Malene Jacobsen

THE MISSING SON — A FAROE ISLAND SAGA

◦◦◦

The *í Lon* house is very near the sandy beach at the end of the Fuglafjørður bay, and the surf is usually very calm, since the bay is protected from the open ocean by neighboring islands. Even though Anna was only three years old, she was allowed to play there.

Reading these letters, I often wonder at the resiliency and strength of young women like Malene, who must raise their children and take care of elderly parents, while their husbands are away at sea for weeks or months at a time. It seems to me that in the Faroese culture, people are careful to support and take care of each other.

◦◦◦

Fuglefjord, 5 April 1920

Dear Brother,

Now that I have your address, I will write to you with pleasure to let you know that we all are well.

The weather has been very bad up to now, so the ships have not been out fishing. Just now they have gone out for fishing. Joen your brother is sailing with Nordlyset, *and I am with a smaller boat. There has not been much fish, but in the last week the boat fished from 500-800 fish each trip.*

Last winter 20 new ships came to the Faroes. They came from different places, such as Sweden, England, Iceland. One of these was sailed down by a German trawler and was sunk on the way from Iceland to Faroes. All the men were saved. I thank you for the post cards you sent to my children.

Loving greetings from me and my family.

Johannes P. Jacobsen

◦◦◦

These three letters, one from each of my father's siblings, were written within a few days of each other. They must have gotten a letter with his new address, and all replied at the same time.

After the war, there was a big increase in shipping traffic in the Faroe Islands and all over the North Atlantic Ocean, but even though the war was over, the fishing ships were not safe from the effects of the war.

∽

Fuglefjord, 22 September 1920

Dear Hans,

I will now write to you and let you know how we are. We are well, and wish you the same. I want to ask you if you would be nice to buy a pair of shoes for me, if they are not too expensive, size 38 or 37. I can not get them here. All the ships from Fuglefjord have come back. Greetings from your parents, sister, and brothers.

Kind regards,
Thomine Poulsen

∽

The envelope for this letter was addressed to the S/S Otta in Bergen, Norway, and then was forwarded to Nice, France. Thomine was about eight years younger than my father, and she had been raised by his parents after her mother died. On my first visit in 1997 she was in very poor health living in a rest home in Fuglafjørður, and she died a few months later.

Even though the war had been over for a year, goods and supplies were still in short supply. I wonder if my father bought the shoes and if he figured out how to convert European shoe sizes to American sizes.

∽

Fuglefjord 13 November 1920

Dear Brother,

Now I will try to write again. I wrote a letter in August and it came back to me again.

The fishing did not give much money this year. We came home again in August from Iceland because it was too dangerous with all the mines, and therefore we did not fish so much. The ship Karen *has sunk because of mines. The ships* Kristine *and* Helene *have also gone down with all the men because of stormy weather on the south coast of Iceland. About 50 fishermen have died on the sea, but none of them are from Fuglefjord and neither are any of them from our family. God saved us.*

Tell me how much money you get with your ship and tell me also when you will come home again. With kind regards from us all.

Joen Fr. Jacobsen

ᘐ

It took a long time for the Faroese economy to recover after the war, and the mines continued to pose a risk to fishing ships. The area south of Iceland has prime fishing waters, so it was an additional economic hardship when ships had to avoid these waters for their own safety.

ᘐ

Fuglefjord 13 December 1920

Dear Brother,

We are well and wish you the same. My dear brother, I have gotten no letter from you. I hear that our parents got a letter from you. I did not know much news, but now it will soon be Christmas, and I will write some words to you.

Regards from my husband. He has much to do. He is sewing sails. Also regards from the boys. They always are asking when you will come home again, and they say to each other that it has been so long since they saw you that they will not know you again.

Lovely regards from your sister.

Malene Hansen

A real Merry Christmas and a happy new year.

LETTERS, 1920-1924

Dear Hans,

I ask you if you can buy me an accordion when you come home again.

Jacob Hansen

～

DEAR UNCLE,

WE WISH TO SEND YOU A POST CARD. WE ARE WELL AND WISH YOU THE SAME.

MAGDA, PETRINA, AND JOEN AND THE LITTLE JACOB

TO HANS JACOBSEN

～

This postcard from the Hansen children was undated, but it must have been written after Petrina was born in 1920 and before Poul Jacob was born in 1922.

～

Fuglefjord, 23 January 1921

Dear Brother,

Thank you for the letter we got from you this month. We are well and wish you the same.

The weather this winter has been good. The fishing has been so bad, worse than we ever had before, and it seems that it will not be good next year. These days everything is expensive here.

Next year I will be captain of Zealous, *but it is difficult to get enough men to come with me.*

I end this letter with kind regards from us all.

Joen Fr. Jacobsen
Fuglefjord

～

THE MISSING SON — A FAROE ISLAND SAGA

Fuglefjord, 21 August 1921

Dear Son,

I will now write to you and let you know how we are. We are tolerably well, and wish from our heart, dear son, that you are well.

We are sorry that you are so cold toward us that you will not send us a photograph of you, and now you are further away from us than you have ever been before. You did not say if we can expect you to come home again. You cannot believe how much we are longing to see you.

Your brother Joen is first chief on Zealous. *We have not heard from them, but from all the other ships from here we know that the fishing has been good. I will send you good greetings from all your relatives here. They all miss you and want you to come home. You cannot believe how nice Anna and Nikoline are. They ask all the time who I am writing to, and when "Ba-Ba" ("papi" or father) is coming. Hannes your brother is home and he wishes you all the best. You have to write to me as soon as possible. I think you now have forgotten to write to me.*

Best wishes from your sister-in-law, because that is who is writing. Loving greetings from all in this house, first and last from your parents,

N. and Joen M. Jacobsen

∽

It is hard to imagine how difficult it was for my grandparents when their youngest son left home and didn't return. I also wonder if they realized how far away he really was and how difficult it would be to return to the Faroe Islands from the Pacific or the Indian Oceans.

∽

Kaloa, 9 April 1922

Dear Parents,

Now I will write you and let you know that I am well and wish you the same. I am sailing with a ship from Kristiana {in Norway} named Remus. *We are sailing on the west coast of America. We are now in Kaloa, a little south of the equator, and it is very hot; here it is never winter, here it is*

64

summer all year long. I cannot say when I am coming home again. Maybe it will not be so long.

    Good wishes,

        Hans Jacobsen

    I cannot give you any address. Also greetings to my sister and brothers.

∞

This is the second letter from my father to his parents that was saved by my cousins. It was over a year between letters from his family. During this time my father sailed mainly in the Pacific Ocean, and his records showed that his travels included four continents – North America, South America, Asia, and Australia.

∞

Fuglefjord, 20 September 1922

Dear Brother,

Some days ago we had the pleasure of getting a letter from you from S/S Bearport.

We are well and with our whole heart we wish you the same. Our old house í Lon is now taken down, and our brother is building a new house across from Skulilsden. It is 10-12 alin with a garret. Our parents live with me until the house is built. There have been many changes since you were here last time. There have been many houses built. Last autumn they started to build a road between Fuglefjord and Saltifjord. This road will be done in 1925. The State will pay 4/5 and the commune 1/5. The road will cost about 180,000 kroner.

The ships have not caught much here in the Faroes, but the ships in Iceland have fished very well. Several ships have come home from Iceland, and they have fished from 30,000-40,000 skippund cod.

The last 2 years I have not been with Faroese ships. I fished with British trawlers, and I have made good money. I now have 5 children, the youngest is ½ year, 2 girls and 3 boys. Our sister has just had a son, who is 1 month old, and our brother has 3 girls, the youngest is 1 month, and they were both baptized yesterday. His name is Poul Jacob and her name Magdalena.

Do you believe that you will ever come to see us again in this world? I will wish that you would hold to Jesus, then you will be happy wherever you wander. Though I could write much more, I have to stop now.

Friendly and loving greetings from your parents and my family. Write again as soon as you can and tell us if you will come home again to the Faroes.

Joh's P. Jacobsen

෴

My father was with the S.S. Bearport from June 1922 through April 1923. The ship was headquartered in Vancouver, making numerous trips to the Far East.

The new house that Joen built is still in the family, and his daughter Petra lived there. *Skulilsden* is a boulder that you can still see near the beach just off of the main street entering Fuglafjørður. Before the road to Fuglafjørður was built, the only way to get to Fuglafjørður was by sea or by walking over mountain passes.

Johannes never mentioned the names of his children in any of the letters to my father, though he did include the names of his new niece and nephew. I'm sure he never suspected that years later this same brother's daughter would be reading these letters trying to find names of her cousins in the Faroe Islands.

My father's parents and brothers and sister were all devout Christians, and they were very concerned that he remain true to the faith in which he was raised. The stationery used for many of the letters had preprinted Bible verses on the top of each page. He also received this post card from Thomine, encouraging him to follow Jesus.

෴

From Thomine Poulsen
To Hans Jacobsen

I wish to send you a little reminder. Go in Jesus arms. He will not push you away. Then you will be safe from the wind. If you have him as a friend, you can let it be stormy, and you will come safely again to the land.

෴

LETTERS, 1920-1924

This next letter from January 1923 was the one that helped me find my cousin Poul Jacob Hansen, and the corrected translation has young Jacob requesting an accordion, not a harmonica.

༄

Fuglefjord 18 January 1923

Dear Brother,

I will write you and let you know how we are. We are well and wish you the same. I want to let you know that I have got a son; his name is Poul Jacob and he is six months old. You have to write soon. Jacob asks if you can buy an accordion for him, but it is so much to ask of you.

I do not know so much news. Nordlyset *sank and all the men died. Three of them were from Fuglefjord, Fredag and 2 young men Martin Georg and Ole Jacob Jacobsen.*

Dear brother, are you never thinking about coming home again. Send us a photo so we can see how you look. We hope to hear from you.

Loving regards from us all, children and Johannes.

From your sister,

Malene Hansen

༄

The ship *Norðlyset* was from Fuglafjørður, and both Johannes and Joen had sailed with this ship off and on from 1905 to 1922. A model of the *Norðlyset* was hanging in the Fuglafjørður church, a reminder to pray for those at sea. During my first visit to the islands, each church I visited had a model of a ship hanging from the peak of the sanctuary as a reminder to pray.

In 1923 Johannes was sailing with *Kristiana,* coming home from Grimsby in very rough weather, when they saw flames in the distance one evening at about 8 pm. After they arrived home they learned that *Norðlyset* had been lost at sea near Grimsby, and that all the men were lost. The flames they saw were most likely from *Norðlyset.*

༄

THE MISSING SON — A FAROE ISLAND SAGA

At Sea – 5 July 1923

Dear Parents,

I will now write and tell you that I am well and wish you the same. I am on board this ship that you can see. We are sailing from San Francisco to Honolulu, and then we shall sail to Australia to a place with the name of Sydney. It is a very nice boat with two propellers and it is sailing 18 miles/ hour. I am Quartermaster, which means that my only job is to steer the ship. Here it is very nice weather, always warm, and the sun shines every day. It has been about two years since I last saw snow. I think that I will freeze when I once again will come home.

> *From Hans Jacobsen*
> *San Francisco, California, U.S.A.*

৶৹

We have a photograph of the *S/S Ventura*, and my father made more than one trip on this ship from San Francisco to Sydney. I know that my father did not like cold or snowy weather, and during the years that I knew him, he never voluntarily made a trip to the snow. San Francisco has rain in the winter and fog in the summer, but no snow, and I suspect that is one reason my father decided to settle there.

৶৹

Fuglefjord (undated, about 20 August 1923)

Dear Brother-in-law,

Now I will take the liberty of writing on my husband's behalf. We were very glad to see the picture of you. Your brother had just gone on the next trip to east Iceland. They have been on south Iceland, too. They have fished 520 skippund. We are tolerably well. Your parents are weak, especially your mother. They have now taken the old house down and they live with us. We now live near Skudles-ten so you can find it when you come home. It is a house made of wood.

We now have three daughters. The youngest was 1 year last Thursday. Her name is Magdalena, like your sister. If we had a photograph of them, then I would have sent one to you. Mina is in the hospital. She visits us often when she is at home.

Dear brother-in-law, we would like for you now to come home again. The door will stay open for you when you come. Write again soon. Anna says that she will go to the post office with the letter, because we have said to her that with the next mail from you she will get a doll from you. She has brought writing paper for me and now she is waiting for the letter, and she will go at once to the post office. She will be 5 years old on Friday. She always goes shopping for me, but your father spoils her. I do not know more to write this time.

You look so educated in the pictures. We got only 2 pictures. If there had been 3, we would have had one for each.

Loving greetings from your sister-in-law,
   Malene Jacobsen

❧

My father finally had his photograph taken in San Francisco in 1923 and had copies made as postcards, and I brought a copy of this photograph to the Faroe Islands, hoping that I would be able find my relatives and show them what my father looked like. One of the most amazing events of my trip was seeing a framed photograph of my father on the wall in the home of one of my relatives, enlarged from the postcard. When I think of the strangeness and improbability of finding my father's family half a world away, eighty years after he left home, the most strange and yet most reassuring event was seeing the photographs of him in my cousins' homes. His family loved him and missed him deeply.

❧

Fuglefjord, 20 August 1923

Dear Brother,

Greetings from Jacob and he thanks you so much for the accordion. You cannot believe how glad he was. Most of the young boys wanted to buy it from him, but he has got the accordion from you and therefore he will not sell it. He is making music from morning to evening. But it seems so sad that I could not find any word from you in the package. I searched through all of the papers, but I did not find anything.

Hans Jacobsen finally had his photo taken in 1923 in San Francisco. This is one of the photos my father sent to his family.

LETTERS, 1920-1924

Dear brother, you have now forgotten how many sisters and brothers you have when you did not send one photograph for each. The first time I saw the picture, I could not believe it was you, but when I look at the picture often, then I can remember how you look. You must also send me a picture. Write again to me and let me know when you will come home again.

Kind regards from us all, and also from the children. Regards from your sister.

Malene Hansen

ᘇ

I was very surprised to read that my father sent an accordion to his nephew Jacob. I think that my father probably sent another photograph to Malene. When I visited Petra, Jacob's widow, she brought out a box of old photos and letters that included the postcard photograph of my father.

ᘇ

Fuglefjord 17 October 1923

Dear Brother,

Thanks to God, I am well and wish you the same. First, I will thank you for the letter I got from you and the pictures you sent.

I am very well. I have built a new house and taken down the old one. We now have a nice home. We have three daughters and my parents also live with us. Mina is in the hospital in Torshavn, and her health is not good. Jacob Martin lives in Vaag on Suderoy, and he is well. I have been fishing this summer and the fishing has been good. The price for the saltfish is now 0,16 kroner per pound. Two years ago it was 0,35 kroner per pound. You can see that times are not easy. There is a big difference in how much we earn. The fish prices are low, and the prices for the materials are still high.

My dear brother, write to me and tell me how much you get and how it is in all the countries you visit. Your parents wish you all the best, and they wish to see you again, and they are all well. I will finish the letter now and wish you all the best.

> *From your brother,*
>> *Joen Fr. Jacobsen*

❦

Fuglefjord 15 Novmeber 1923

Dear Brother,

I will now write some words and let you know how we are. We are well, and wish you the same.

Thank you for the letter. We are very glad to hear from you. I did not know much to tell you. You must not forget to write. You know that we are glad to hear from you. Regards from Jacob. He has now been confirmed. Regards from your parents. They are well. Maybe they are writing now. I wish you were home for the Christmas time. Merry Christmas and a happy new year.

Greetings from your sister, husband, and the children.

> *Malene Hansen*

❦

Fuglefjord, 17 July 1924

Dear Son and Brother,

With pleasure I will write to you and let you know that I am well and we all are well.

I have not been out fishing with small boats since 1916. I have been with trawlers, 2-3 voyages every spring-time fishing saltfish. Joen our brother is master of the ship Zealous. *It was not a good voyage last spring to South Iceland. Ten days after they left the Faroes they sailed on land, and the men were saved. This trip he was the second master. It is not easy to live here in the Faroe Islands, goods are expensive and the income is not enough. The fishery for the South Iceland has failed. The summer is bad, rainy and windy, and there are no fish in the islands.*

The ship owner S. P. Petersen has gone bankrupt. The fishermen can maybe only get 40% of their money. His sons have taken over the shop.

Malene Hansen and her youngest son Poul Jacob at his confirmation at age 14.

I now have 6 children, 4 boys and 2 girls, and we are all well. I am sad that I have no photograph to send you of my family.

Write to me as soon as possible, and tell me about what you see, and I think that is not so little. Please send me a photograph of you. Lastly, I wish that God may bless you and your job out in the great world, and if we do not to meet each other again in this world, I wish that we will meet in Heaven.

Loving wishes from Father, Mother and all your family.

Job's P. Jacobsen

∽

Johannes and Margretha had seven children, and shortly after Sam, the youngest, was born, Margretha died. Her older sister Susanna Katrina came to help take care of the children, and eventually Johannes and Susanna were married.

This is the last letter that my father received from his family. I have a note in my mother's writing that my father last wrote home in 1924, but he received no answer. He assumed his parents were dead. By this time, I think that my father's family knew that he would not return to the Faroe Islands.

GETTING ACQUAINTED

OVERLEAF: Sheep graze beside the road to Fuglafjørður near Kambsdalur, with mountains on the islands of Kalsoy and Kunoy visible across the bay. ➤

Fuglafjørður, October 2007: *Let me start by saying that at home in America, I am quite an adequate cook, maybe even a good cook. People eat the food I prepare and say nice things about it. However, I find cooking in a foreign country to be a challenge. There are countless ways that something may go wrong, and I keep finding new ways.*

Potatoes are a staple in the Faroese diet – not mashed potatoes and gravy, not baked potatoes with butter and sour cream, but boiled new potatoes. While living in the Faroe Islands for a year in 2005-06, I realized that I really wanted some good American mashed potatoes with gravy. I boiled some small new potatoes from Denmark, and then tried to figure out how to mash them. I didn't have a potato masher, but I did have a very small hand mixer with a single beater attachment. As I beat the potatoes with my little hand mixer, I realized that they were not becoming light and fluffy, like American potatoes, but rather they were smooth and glossy. I discovered that you can make very good wallpaper glue by beating small new potatoes from Denmark with an electric mixer. Apparently new potatoes have a lot more gluten than the large russet potatoes I use in America, and beating them turns them into glue. That day I ate potato flavored glue with gravy. It tasted pretty good.

One day on a visit to my local FK grocery store, I saw a box on the shelf with a picture of a bowl of mashed potatoes topped with chopped chives and a basil leaf. So this is how you are supposed to make mashed potatoes! I bought the box. Note that I have been studying very hard to learn Faroese, and I know the name of many foods in Faroese. However, like most packaged foods here, the mashed potatoes were packaged in Denmark and had instructions in Danish. I don't have a Danish dictionary, so my method for reading something in Danish is to stare at the words for a long time while I try to think of a word in some other language that is similar. Sometimes it works. The name on the box with the picture of a bowl of mashed potatoes said KARTOFFELMOS. It has been a few years, but I remembered that the German word for potato is something like "kartoffel," and I could imagine that MOS might mean "mash." Kogende vand must be "cooked water," so I cooked some water. One brev must be an envelope (and the French for "letter" is something like "breve", which goes into an envelope) of kartoffelmospulver, or potato mash powder (which comes from pulverizing potatoes). Hurrah! By adding hot water to the package I did get mashed potatoes that were quite tasty and fluffy like American potatoes. I have a few other phrases in my Danish-English cooking dictionary for Faroese food. These are from a box of Tomatsuppe, soup from another pulverized vegetable.

GETTING ACQUAINTED

- *Kog op under omrøring: My literal translation is "cook up under roaring." If you consider that a roaring river looks like boiling water, this is clearly the equivalent of "heat to boiling."*

- *Småkoge i 5 minutter: Literally this sounds like "small cook in 5 minutes," which I translate to "simmer for 5 minutes."*

- *Rør rundt af og til: Rundt looks like "round" or "around," and if rør is related to a roaring river, my guess is that this is "stir vigorously now and again."*

- *I will let you try to translate this one without any help: Tips til servering.*

Recently, I tried to roast a leg of lamb with roasted vegetables (potatoes, carrots, and onions). It was a little more complicated than adding boiling water, but actually it did seem quite simple. I put rosemary and garlic on the lamb and put it in the oven to start cooking. Then I got the vegetables ready, and added them about an hour later. When I opened the oven door, the oven wasn't warm! I am fortunate enough to have two ovens in my little house, but I had turned on the wrong oven. I wanted to turn the oven to about 350 degrees F, but I couldn't find my conversion chart. I set the temperature to 200 degrees C, and hoped for the best. Oh, the poor vegetables! I cooked them at 400 degrees F for an extra hour (thanks to the oven mix-up), and they all had a nice rich dark crust on the bottom.

With international cooking, maybe I should stick to adding cooked water to packages of pulverized vegetables.

Chapter 6 – Getting Acquainted

During the next few days, I got better acquainted with my cousins and their families, and I also got to see a little more of the Faroe Islands. Most of the time I had no idea of what we were going to do next, but I did my best to be flexible and took whatever happened as an adventure. I think that sometimes my relatives didn't have the English vocabulary to explain our plans, sometimes the cultural differences resulted in wrong expectations, and sometimes I think they simply forgot to tell me in English about our plans, forgetting, for the moment, that I didn't understand what they had just been discussing in Faroese.

One cultural difference between the US and the Faroes made it more difficult for me to get to know my relatives. In America, even young children are taught how to make introductions. This doesn't happen in the Faroe Islands, and it was very rare for me to be introduced to someone. This put me at a distinct disadvantage, since many people knew who I was, but nearly everyone was new to me. I got in the habit of introducing myself, expecting that people would tell me their names in return, but it was soon clear that introductions were not a part of the Faroese culture. If I wanted to know who someone was, I would just have to ask them. Occasionally, someone would tell me who another person was, but if I wanted to meet them, I would have to go by myself to talk to them.

I received many invitations to visit relatives, and most of these invitations were phrased in English as an invitation for coffee. I was surprised by the wide variety of foods that are included in an invitation to come for coffee. It might be a meal – breakfast or lunch. It might be an elaborate spread of desserts, or maybe pancakes with a lot of different toppings, or only cookies. Fortunately, it wasn't ever just coffee. In America, invitations are usually more specific. "Come for lunch." "Come for dinner." "Come for a barbecue." "Come for dessert." "Come for light refreshments." It seems like all of these were included in the invitation to "Come for coffee".

Most Faroese people drink a lot of coffee, and they drink it at any time of the day. I usually have coffee with breakfast, but coffee later in the day keeps me awake at night. This doesn't seem to be much of a problem in the Faroe Islands, where coffee is served in the morning, with lunch, in the afternoon, with dinner, and always late at night. No one ever served decaffeinated coffee, and, in fact, it has only recently become available in the grocery stores. Since I was trying to fit in, learn the culture, and be accommodating, I often drank the coffee that was offered. Then I lay awake half the night staring at the ceiling, the result of jet-lag and too many cups of coffee.

Jutta handled all of the invitations and organized my schedule, and sometimes we visited several relatives in one day. Monday morning we were invited to coffee by my cousin Petra, who lived in the home built by my father's brother Joen in the early 1920's. Four of my cousins were there, Petra, her brother Aksel, her sister Ninna, and Poul Jacob. We sat at the breakfast table for a long time while my cousins talked in Faroese. Later, I asked Bernhard what they were talking about, and he told me that they were very happy to learn that my father had lived a long and full life and that I had come to the Faroes to find his family.

In the afternoon, first I did some shopping and then I went sight-seeing. Since I was staying with relatives instead of in a hotel, I decided to use some of my hotel money to buy Faroese wool sweaters. I selected a traditional Faroese dark brown sweater with silver buttons for myself, and I also got sweaters for my husband and children. A very generous relative insisted on paying for all of the sweaters, so I still had all of my hotel money unspent.

GETTING ACQUAINTED

After my shopping was done, Gunnleyg and Esmann took me on a sight-seeing tour of the southern part of Eysturoy, stopping often for me to take photographs. Whenever I saw something of interest, I asked Esmann to stop so I could take a picture, forgetting that he not only didn't understand any English, but that he was also hard of hearing. Gunnleyg encouraged me to shout "STOP," rather than asking politely. Once Esmann understood me, he would stop and back up so I could take my picture. Often the scenery that I found beautiful or unusual and wanted to photograph was something that my relatives took for granted, because they saw it every day. I don't think they ever understood why I took so many pictures of creeks, waterfalls, green hillsides, yellow flowers, bays, and the ocean.

Sometimes I found it frustrating that I couldn't communicate with my cousins. I spent a lot of time with Esmann and Gunnleyg, and Gunnleyg spoke English quite well, but Esmann not at all. One day Esmann and I were alone in the car, and we tried to have a conversation. In about 10 minutes of talking, we successfully communicated two things. First, "It is raining," which we said while pointing at the raindrops on the windshield, and second, "Friday I am going to Mykines" ("Friday, Mykines"). After that we both gave up trying to talk and just drove in silence.

That evening, after dinner with Poul Jacob and Jutta, we watched on television as Hong Kong was turned over to China. This was the only time during my trip that I was at all aware of what was going on in the outside world.

Tuesday morning we drove to Hellur, a small scenic village that is built on a rocky ledge between the water's edge and the base of a tall mountain. It is just over the mountain pass north of Fuglafjørður, but to get there we took the long way around, driving south over two passes, then north along the edge of the bay, up the hill over another pass, and finally down into another valley beside another bay.

Hellur is one of the words that is confusing to Americans. On paper it looks like a very simple two-syllable word, but when it is pronounced it sounds like a different word. When I would try to say it, people would look at me blankly, because I was saying it wrong. It was years before I learned that two *l*'s sound like *tl*. *Vágar* is another word

83

that I finally gave up on, and I know I am not alone. Most foreigners soon learn to call it "the island with the airport," because when we say it, Faroese people either look blank like they don't understand us, or they correct us and say some other word that doesn't seem to be related at all to the written word. I was never sure whether I was saying the wrong word or only pronouncing it wrong. As an American, I would expect *Vágar* and *Vágur* to be pronounced nearly the same. In Faroese, the first sounds like **VOH-ahr** and the second sounds like **VWAH-vuhr**. My Faroese/English dictionary has twenty pages of rules for pronouncing the Faroese language, and to make this even more confusing, the rules are based on the British pronunciation of English, not the American. I have found that it helps to carry a map when traveling in the Faroes, so I can point to the location where I want to go.

In the evening we were invited to Diana's home for dinner, where I expected a quiet evening with Diana, Poul Jacob, and Jutta. However, the evening was anything but quiet. Diana lived in a small house near the end of the single road that skirted the far edge of the Fuglafjørður bay, overlooking the fish factory and the commercial dock. The main level of the house was divided into two small rooms, a kitchen and a living/dining room which had a table on one side and a small sofa with two easy chairs on the other. When we arrived, the small house was already crowded with Diana's family – her children, grandchildren, spouses, and one great-grand child. It was a noisy, talkative crowd. Those of the younger generation were all fluent in English, and I always had someone to talk with.

This meal was the first time I experienced the Faroese custom of serving a meal with several different seatings. At home we would have had some people sitting around the dining table, another group around the kitchen table, and others sitting on the sofa and chairs in the living room, so everyone could eat at the same time. Instead, the small table was set with eight place settings of Diana's best china, and eight of us sat down to dinner. When we were done, the grandchildren cleared the table, re-set it with the second best china, and the rest of the crowd had their dinner, while others started washing dishes. Later Lillian, Bernhard, and their son arrived to join us for dessert, so now there were eighteen noisy people in the small house, and three of them

GETTING ACQUAINTED

were called Poul Jacob. Two of the children came from playing soccer games as part of the annual Fuglafjørður festival, and win or lose, everyone received a medal. Looking out of Diana's window we could see rowboats in the bay training for the upcoming races.

Fuglafjørður was busy preparing for the annual Warm Springs or Varmakelda festival, named for the warm spring south of the town on the edge of the bay. On Wednesday morning Poul Jacob and I walked over to the school where festival officials were making preparations for an art exhibition. The television crew, who had come to film the exhibit, heard about the long-lost cousin from America and arranged to interview Poul Jacob and me. We showed them some of the letters from Poul Jacob's mother written to my father, and some of the photographs of my father, including the one from my cousin's house in Fuglafjørður. Seven or eight minutes of our interview were included in the evening news, and several times I met people who recognized me from the television program, even in later trips to the Faroes.

Many people came to Fuglafjørður for the festival, and it was the custom for residents to open their homes for guests, even for people they didn't know. In the evening we had dinner at the home of Jóhan Heri and Marjun, who were hosting a couple from Norway who had come for the festival. Sometimes I felt awkward at mealtimes, since Faroese customs were still new to me, and I would have preferred to watch what other people did and then copy them; but often I was treated as the guest of honor and was encouraged to serve myself first. Marjun served a delicious, rich looking dessert covered with whipped cream and nuts. When I tried to spoon some onto my plate, I was unsuccessful. I discovered that it was ice cream, very firmly frozen ice cream, and I needed a knife rather than a spoon.

In Fuglafjørður, there were very few street signs, and few of the houses had numbers on them. I had trouble finding Jóhan Heri's house more than once, even though I was sure I knew where I was going. The following year in 1998, I visited the Faroes with my brother, and I walked with him up to Jóhan Heri's house, assuring everyone that I knew the way. We walked up and down the street several times until Marjun finally saw us from the window and called to us. I made a mental note to myself that their house was black with green windows, so I could find it next time.

The following summer I had a slightly different problem, again on the way to Jóhan Heri's house. My husband Curtis came with me to the Faroes in 1999, and once again I was walking up to Jóhan Heri's house, telling everyone that this time I could find the right place. As we approached the house, I assured my husband that the custom in the Faroes is to walk right in the front door into the entry way, call out "Hello," and take off coats, sweaters, boots, and scarves. By then, the host or hostess would be there to welcome us. It also seemed strange to us to have coats, sweaters, and scarves in the middle of summer. Unfortunately for me, Jóhan Heri was in the process of painting the house, so I walked past his house and into the front door of their neighbor's black house. Once inside the door, I knew I was in the wrong place, because the entry way had no staircase. My husband was mortified that we had just walked into a stranger's house, but the kind woman who lived there pointed us to the house next door. Looking back from this perspective, we could see the one wall of Jóhan Heri's house that was not yet painted; and it was, as I had remembered, black with a green window.

Thursday morning I set off for a two day car trip with three cousins, Diana, her niece Margretha, and her nephew's wife Áshild. Neither Diana nor Margretha spoke English, and in the car I often dosed with the sound of Faroese voices in my ears. After I returned home, I would occasionally dream that I heard people speaking Faroese, but I still didn't know what anyone was saying. We were going to Sandoy to visit Anna Katrin, but we made many stops along the way.

We spent some time in Tórshavn, and I got to see a little more of the city that I had visited by mistake during my first hours in the Faroe Islands. We visited the history museum, the art museum, and the Nordic House performance hall; and we went shopping in the town center and also at the SMS shopping center with its 25-30 shops. A sign over one shop in the town center caught my attention – *Hans N. Jacobsen Bóksavn,* a bookstore that seemed to be named after my father. In both the art gallery and the Nordic House we listened to visiting choirs rehearsing for concerts later in the day, part of the annual summer concert series.

Magnus Cathedral in Kirkjubøur was built about 1300, and it served as the cathedral of the Faroe Islands until the Reformation.

We left Tórshavn and crossed the hills to the western side of the island, heading south to the little town of Kirkjubøur. During the Middle Ages, this small town was the cultural and religious center of the islands, and it has several striking and fascinating buildings. The landscape is dominated by the ruins of the Saint Magnus Cathedral, built of gray stone, with tall narrow arched openings for windows facing the ocean, and only clouds for a roof and ferns and mosses growing from the stonework. Construction on the cathedral began in the late thirteenth century, but apparently the building was never completed. The small white parish church nearby sits right at the edge of the water, and much of the ancient churchyard has been washed away by the sea. This church has been used as a house of worship continuously since 1100, though the building has been rebuilt several times. The Bible on the altar is dated 1585, and many pages are ornamented with large decorative capitals and delicate paintings. For many years, the pews in the church had elaborately carved pew ends, each with carved bas relief figures and a coat of arms, but these pews ends are currently in a museum in Tórshavn.

The third building of note is the 900 year old log smoke-room that is now a museum. The log building seemed out of place in a landscape with no trees. The building was originally built in Norway and was later moved to Kirkjubøur. Each log was carefully marked with its location in the building, the building was dismantled, the logs were towed from Norway to the Faroe Islands, and the building was reassembled in Kirkjubøur in the 1500's. The small house is filled with many artifacts from both Norwegian and Faroese history. I was particularly struck by the low stools; each was the vertebra of a whale.

The farmhouse in Kirkjubøur has been the home of the farmer since 1550, and earlier it was the home of the Faroese bishop. The old smoke room dates from about 1100.

GETTING ACQUAINTED

Áshild seemed to know people wherever we went, and she introduced us to the Farmer's wife from the adjacent property, who gave us a tour of their private home and told us many stories from Faroese history. The most famous legend tells of a young Faroese girl in the twelfth century who was taken to Norway to be a part of the king's household. She became pregnant with the king's child and then escaped from Norway to Kirkjubøur to keep her child from being killed. When her son was born he was hidden in the cliffs and mountains above Kirkjubøur. After the death of the Norwegian king, the young man returned to Norway, where he provoked a bloody coup and became king. The Faroe Islands have a long, bloody history, and they were often used as a pawn in battles between Norway and Denmark. Another Faroese legend told the history of the small Kirkjubøur church. In about 1100 an elderly Catholic bishop came to the Faroe Islands, set up the Faroese Bishopric in Kirkjubøur, and established the small church. As time went on, it was difficult for him to keep up with his duties, and a local Faroese woman assumed most of the duties of running the church and the parish. After the elderly bishop died, he was replaced by a young man who resented having a woman running his church, so he had her killed.

We took the evening ferry to Sandoy, and then drove across the island to Anna Katrin's home, which is isolated even by Faroese standards, all by itself far from town on a narrow road. The property includes a row of buildings near the sea: barn, boat house, storage sheds, garage, and their home. The family had built the main part of their home about ten years earlier. Anna Katrin, her husband Torstein, and their two young children sailed to Norway in their boat, cut down some trees, loaded them onto the boat, brought them back to the Faroe Islands, milled the logs into lumber, and built their house – quite an amazing feat by American standards.

Torstein is a dentist, and he and Anna Katrin were preparing to sail to Greenland, where he would spend the year sailing around the coastline, examining the teeth of all of the school children. They have two children, a son who worked in Tórshavn, whom we met on the ferry, and a daughter Durita, who was skipper of a boat sailing around the world. After she finished high school, her father bought her a boat and then refurbished it for the trip. Torstein and Anna Katrin sailed with

89

her to Portugal, making sure the vessel was sea-worthy for such a long trip. They joined the boat again in Puerto Rico, sailing through the Panama Canal, spending time in the Galapagos Islands, and sailing to Tahiti before returning home. They had arrived home only a few days before I came to the Faroes. Their home was filled with many artifacts from their trips to various parts of the world; a tortoise shell from the Galapagos joined several narwhale teeth, reindeer skins from Norway, and rams' horns from the Faroes. Several years later, on another visit to the Faroes, I met another relative, who had sailed with Durita for about six months, from Tahiti to Indonesia. He showed us photos of his trip through the South Pacific islands, as well as a copy of Durita's book documenting the three year voyage.

For dinner that night I had my first taste of pilot whale meat, which had been salted for preservation. I wasn't very fond of the meat. It didn't seem to have any grain, was almost gelatinous, and was very

Stone Viking houses in Húsavík were built about 1450. The Vikings turned their boats upside-down over the stone walls for easy waterproof roofs.

rich. Torstein, Anna Katrin, and their son all spoke English, and we stayed up late talking. At midnight we went for a walk along the road, going south even farther from civilization. As the skies finally darkened, the birds on the cliffs below us became silent, and in the misty fog the whole world seemed muffled and remote. Apparently the birds sleep for only an hour or two at night during the summer, and wake up again when the skies become light.

In the morning after breakfast, we walked around Anna Katrin's property. Broken oyster shells were scattered over the rocky shoreline. It seems that oystercatcher birds really do catch shellfish, and then they drop their catch on the rocks so they can eat the meat inside. After lunch Anna Katrin came with us on a drive around the island. We saw the 500 year old Viking settlement at Húsavík, where several stone houses stood on a low ridge above the wide bay and sandy beach. The Vikings built the houses with gently curved walls, and then they used their up-side-down boats for waterproof roofs, providing quick protection during the long, cold winters. I walked barefoot along the beach by myself and put my feet in the cold Atlantic waters. No one else was willing to join me. The water was achingly cold, much colder than the Northern California Pacific Ocean beaches.

On the way back to Anna Katrin's house we stopped so I could watch a sheep-shearing. The noise from the sheep was deafening. I explained to the sheep shearers that I was from America, and this was the first time I had seen anyone shear a sheep.

On the way home we stopped at the radio station in Tórshavn for my interview with Jógvan Árge. His voice was very familiar to me, since even during my short visit I had heard him announce many soccer games on the radio. We talked for about an hour and a half, and he made arrangements to get copies of my father's letters and photos from a relative in Fuglafjørður.

Back in Fuglafjørður, I joined Áshild and her family for dinner, and she served me yet another favorite Faroese dish, fish balls that her mother had just made, using grated fish, grated onions, and fat from the stomach of a sheep. My stomach hadn't yet recovered from the boiled whale meat, though under other conditions I might have enjoyed the fish balls. Her husband was home from his most recent fishing trip, and he showed me a video of the prawn trawler he works on. His teenage daughter had what I would consider a very unusual summer job. She had spent two months with him on the trawler during her school holiday, working in the processing/freezing plant on the ship.

During the past few years, some of my friends have commented to me on how adventuresome I was to travel by myself to the Faroe Islands without knowing the language or knowing anyone there. However, I feel rather cautious and prudent, when I hear about the adventures of some of my Faroese relatives.

Tiny wild orchids, as big as the tip of my thumb, are scattered over the grassy hillsides during the summer. ➤

Fuglafjørður, May 2009: *Tuesday was a perfect, beautiful spring day in the Faroe Islands – not a cloud in the deep blue sky, not a breath of wind, and only warm sunshine. I walked along the edge of the Fuglafjørður Bay, past the little brown house where I used to live and through the lower fields where the ewes were grazing, to the end of the road near the dump. After I passed the last house, I noticed how quiet it was. There were no people, no cars, no wind, and no noise – only green grass, blue sky, and deep blue water.*

Soon I realized that it wasn't exactly silent, but that I could hear, from time to time, some of the quiet sounds of spring. First, I heard a rooster crowing, from the chicken house way up the road. Then a single ewe bleated, up near the top of the hill. As I passed sheep near the road, I could hear the sounds of the grass tearing as they were grazing. There was the high-pitched bleating of a single lamb, calling its mother. I heard the distinctive call of an oystercatcher, and I could hear the beat of his wings as he flew from one field to another. Far up the hillside a truck rumbled past on the main road, but I could barely hear it. The cars I couldn't hear at all. Occasionally, I could hear the sound of water trickling in one of the small creeks, still flowing since the last rain. Passing the waterfall, I heard a louder sound of splashing water. A small motorboat sailed out to the salmon fisheries at the far end of the bay. In the distance was the call of another bird. Where the road dipped down near the bay, I could hear the surf lapping gently against the shore. Three ducks were softly grumbling while they were eating on the hillside. Walking back to my car, even the sheep seemed to be taking their afternoon naps, resting silently in the fields.

It is spring in the Faroe Islands.

Chapter 7 – Love Letters

When my family discovered the letters from the Faroe Islands after my father's death, we were frustrated by the fact that we couldn't read them, and we didn't know anyone who could. Several years later my brother talked to a Danish acquaintance, who gave him a rough translation of a few of the letters, but she had difficulty translating them because they written in an old-fashioned Danish. As time passed, the letters were put aside and ignored. When I decided to visit the Faroe Islands, I retrieved the letters from my brother and brought them along with me.

During my first weekend in Fuglafjørður, Jóhan Heri made copies of the letters for my cousins as well as a few slides for the family reunion party. The next day, he told me he had stayed up nearly all night reading the letters, and he found them very moving, saying, "There is quite a love story there." About half of the letters were from Maren, a young woman who was engaged to my father. Jóhan Heri read a few excerpts from Maren's letters to me, but I didn't know the whole story until a year later when he gave me a rough hand-written translation. I agree with him; it was quite a love story. Maren corresponded frequently with my father from 1917 through 1923, always hoping he would return to her. Her letters were filled with details about people and events in Fuglafjørður and the Faroe Islands, and they expressed her longing for his return.

THE MISSING SON — A FAROE ISLAND SAGA

Fuglefjord, 15 April 1917

My Dear Sweetheart,

Today it is a great pleasure for me to write to you, my dear friend, and thank you for the letter. I was very glad to get it. You cannot believe how happy I was when I received the letter, for I had heard no word from you since you left, and nobody knew if you were to come back or not, and then I was confused when so long a time had passed.

With all my heart, dear friend, nobody but God knew how much I have thought about you since you left. Every night when I go to bed, I pray to God and beg him to walk with you wherever you go, and that he may let his light make your way bright, and may good luck follow you where you go, and preserve you from the dangers that are around you.

My unforgettable friend, you must not believe that I will ever forget you, no I never will. You are the first I have had so much love for, and there is nobody on the earth that I love more than you. I hope you never will fall away from me. If you fall away from me, then I have nothing to live for. I wish that God will make us strong to be loyal toward each other. Hans, you have to come back again. I do not think it is good for you to sail in the restless world. The person who can be away from the restless places, he can be glad. My loving friend, you have to come back. I beg you. I wish you were here tonight, then how happy I would be, but you are so far away, my dear friend. I think so much about you in this troubled time, but I know that God, who is over us, will find us whether we are we are on the sea or on the land. But it is best to be in our native country among our friends and those we love.

I have heard that Alexander Joensen will come back again. If I knew his address, then I would write it for you, but I do not know the address.

With all my heart, dear friend, I will never forget you, and you must not think that I am unfaithful toward you. Many people say to me that I have been so holy since you left. I never go to dances, and when I do go to the dance hall, I am always thinking about you and how you are. I know that for men who are sailing, it is not always easy for them, they often have to see the dead before their eyes.

Dear friend, I have to stop writing now. With friendly and loving regards. I wish that roses may grow on your way. And the word I write to you is forget-me-not.

Good-bye my friend. May God in Heaven be your escort. I wish that I will yet again see the same friend that is gone from me. Greetings with a full heart from your faithful friend,
    Maren

❦

This letter was dated five months after my father left the Faroe Islands. Maren was a very devout Christian, and she often mentioned praying for my father's safety and that he would remain true to the Christian faith of his upbringing. She was very articulate in expressing the loneliness and hardship of families and friends who must be separated because of the necessity of earning a living at sea, and during the war, it was especially difficult for families at home. Maren's faith in God gave her great comfort.

❦

Fuglefjord, 15 April 1917

My Unforgettable Friend,

    Now I will tell you with pleasure that I am well and I hope you are the same. Lena your sister has been in the hospital in Klaksvik, and she was there for 8 weeks. She had a big operation. There were two doctors, Fysekus came from Torshavn. Now she has come home again and she is healthy again, but she cannot work yet. Danielle, my sister, is now helping her. Johannes is fishing, and she cannot be alone. Edward is also ill. The doctor said that he should get out of bed and go out into the fresh air. If he cannot walk, then he should sit in a chair.

    Davine, the poor thing, God help me, she was ill. She had mumps. Then she got a cold and when she recovered, she lost her son. She didn't sleep for many nights, and then she went mad. The doctor came to see her, but he could do nothing. There had to be four people with her the first days because she was so desperate.

She tried to hurt herself and others. But then she became calmer, so they only needed three women to take care of her, and then only two. There always had to be two people around her, day and night, and people from Fuglefjord were asked to sit with her. I have also been sitting with her. She was staying at Poul Andreas, but now she is with her parents. Now her parents are taking care of her themselves. Now she is calm and she is getting out of bed, but she is still crazy. Her mind hasn't come back. She isn't getting better. She is like a small child. She doesn't speak, but when they ask her to say some words, she can repeat them.

On Shrovetide there was a soccer match between Eide and Fuglefjord. Eide was the winner, 1-0. Kristian should have played, but when Davine was sick, he could not, and he didn't go to the dance in the evening either. He is by her side day and night. It seems that Kristian loves Davine very much and that the love is burning in his heart. When we were sitting with Davine, I thought that it was very difficult to see those you love with such troubles. But now things are going better with Edward. It is the same sickness he has always had. Johannes, your brother, is not fishing. They are repairing the ship. Joen, your brother, is on the south of Iceland with the ship Nordlyset. *Now I have nothing more to tell you. I will write again soon. Please excuse me that the letter is not so beautifully written. I had to write in a hurry.*

From your unforgettable friend,
Maren

&

These two letters apparently were written on the same date. The first was her personal expression of love and concern. The second was filled with news of family and friends. Maren kept my father informed of all that went on in the town.

Klaksvík is the second largest city in the Faroe Islands, with a population of nearly 5,000, and it has a large, well-protected harbor, making it a major shipping center. The city is on the southern tip of Borðoy, to the east of Eysturoy. This is where Lena was hospitalized for her surgery. There are two hospitals in the Faroe Islands, one in Klaksvík, the other in Tórshavn.

&

Fuglefjord, 20 May 1917

My Dear Sweetheart,

I will now write a word to you and let you know that I am well, and I wish you the same. I do not have much news to tell you.

Lena, your sister, is now well. With Davine it is the same, nobody can get her out of bed. The doctor tells her that she must get up and go outdoors, but she will not. Edward is not doing especially well. He is often outdoors, but he is not able to go out fishing again this year.

My unforgettable friend, you cannot believe how much I am thinking about you, and I wish you were here by my side tonight, and I would be so happy and glad. Yes, I have thought much about you since you left. I do not think that you are so well now when times are so bad. Here we can't complain because we are lacking nothing. The Lord is trying us. If it is not good for us, it is our own fault, because we are living without thinking about the Lord. I would wish that the confused world would be good again.

Poul from Andefjord sailed to Copenhagen this winter with a ship from Klaksvik, and they are just coming back. He will come to Fuglefjord tonight with the mail boat from Klaksvik. His father has come here to meet him. They have been so afraid for him because it is so dangerous, but now they are glad that he has come home. My dear, how glad I would be if it were you that came tonight, but you are so far away. I wish that God will let us meet each other again. I am praying to God that he shall hold his hand over you.

My dear, you have to write to me again, as soon as you are able to do it. I am longing so much to hear from you. I have sent one letter before this.

Now I shall close this letter with friendly and warm greetings. I will never forget you as long as I live. There is no one in the world that I love more than you. You must excuse the bad handwriting, because I wrote in a hurry.

From your never forgetting friend,
Maren

∾

Fuglefjord, 25 June 1917

My Dear Sweetheart,

I will now write some words to you and let you know that I am well and I wish the same for you. Thank you for the letter that I got from you. I was very happy when I got the letter. I have waited such a long time, and I thought that you were not alive; but now that I know that you are well I am happy.

My dear friend, you asked about the Faroe ships that were sunk in the Southern Bank. Nine boats were sunk, but all the men were saved. It was nice weather, but the men were in lifeboats for 30 hours. One of the boats, Beinir, *belongs to S. P. Petersen. Other boats were* Isabella, Britannia, *and I do not know the names of the others. It was very alarming before we heard that the crews had been saved.*

My dear friend, it is still the same with Davine. Kristian her husband is always by her side and he is not interested in others. Edward is now well. There is not much to tell you. Everything is the same. There is one thing I should tell you. Niklas Kristiansen is now married to a girl who was working in their house. Johan Medardus from Hallerne is going to marry a girl from Klaksvik. I don't know about any other engagements.

My dear sweetheart, you have to keep writing to me. Letters from you are the only thing that can make me happy. My dear friend, I will never be disloyal toward you. You cannot believe how much I love you. The love is burning inside me, and my thoughts are always with you. I will never forget you.

My dear darling, I hope that God will let us see each other again with love and happiness. My dear friend, you must excuse me because I have no more time to write tonight. The mail is going out now, but I will write again soon. I have to stop now.

With kind regards from your darling who will be faithful until death,
    Maren,
Write again soon. May God hold his hand over you.
Regards from Sigga i Tovuni.

∽

Fuglefjord, 22 July 1917

My Dear Sweetheart,

I cannot keep from writing a letter to you when I know that a boat is sailing, and I wish for you to get it. This is the next letter since I last got a letter from you, and I wish to know how you are. I cannot believe that you have forgotten to write. Maybe you do not have enough time, but when you have, I think you will write to me, dear friend. You are always in my thoughts, every

LOVE LETTERS

night and every day. Every time my eyes are open, I am thinking about you. You may tell me how you are and when you will come home again.

One month ago, the ship Beskytteren *came from Bergen, and I thought that you would come with the ship, but you were not there. You are my friend. You are my best friend of my heart, and never, in this life, shall I forget you. Where ever you will be, my love is with you, and may the great God keep you.*

I have no time to write more tonight because it is dark and I cannot see the lines. The mail boat is leaving and I didn't know it ahead of time or I would have written sooner.

Good wishes from your own friend,
  Maren
You must write again.

∽

Mail to and from the Faroe Islands was very sporadic during the war, and the mail boats could not keep to a regular schedule. Hans was sailing with Norwegian ships during this period, but he was seldom in any port for very long. We have a photo of his ship *Guri* from 1917, which had a home port of Stavanger, Norway.

∽

Lervig, 30 July 1917

My beloved friend,

Now I will write to you and thank you for the letter that I have read with great pleasure. It was nice to hear that you are well, my friend. Your mother is ill. The doctor says that she is very ill. But I wish that the Lord may make her well again. It is not good news to hear that your mother is sick, because I know that you love your mother, and she also loves you. May the Lord allow that you will see each other again.

My dear friend, I am working in Lervig for a short time. If you write to me, you have to send the letter to Fuglefjord. My sweetheart, you must not think that I will forget you. As long as my heart is beating in my breast, I will not forget you, my dear. I will never have so much love for another person

Hans Jacobsen stands on the left, with crew members from the Norwegian ship Guri *in 1917.*

LOVE LETTERS

than I do for you, and I will not have any other than you. You must never think that I am unfaithful to you, my real loving friend. Tonight I am alone in my room, with peaceful thoughts. I think about you, my love, and how happy we would be if tonight you were by my side, and I could rest in your arms, but you are so far away. I will be happy when you come home again. It feels so long to wait. You must write to me. I have only gotten three letters from you since you left. You must excuse me for the last letter that I wrote in a hurry. I didn't know about the boat that was going until the last minute.

My dear friend, there is not so much news from home, but the ships have been to Iceland, and they have had a good catch. Johannes, your brother, has not been to Iceland. He has fished here in the Faroes. I will also tell you that Jacob Thomsen has had a son. My dear friend, you have to send a photo of yourself. It would be a great pleasure for me to look at.

I will stop now. Loving greetings from your faithful friend, the one who will never forget you.

> *Maren,*
> *You must write again. Good bye and live well.*

∽

Lervík is a small town not far from Fuglafjørður. Today it can be reached by a road that tunnels under the mountain, but at the time of this letter, travel was by boat or by a narrow footpath that skirted the mountainous headlands.

∽

Fuglefjord 16 December 1917

My Dear Sweetheart,

I will now write to you. I am well and wish the same for you. Now Malene and Joen your brother are married. It was the 10th of this month. They did not have any wedding party. There were only their brothers and sisters. In the evening we danced the wedding dance, and after that I was invited home with them to eat, but I felt so lonely, because I was missing you, my love, by my side. If you were here it would be a nice night. My thoughts were with you all the time. It was very difficult to go into your parent's home.

103

Your mother is always so kind to me, and I think it is because she knows that we are engaged.

My sweetheart, you cannot think how much I am thinking about you, my loving friend. I wish that you were here tonight, but you are so far away, and there is nobody but you who can make me happy - you my sweetheart. You must not think that I will forget you. No I never will forget you, as long as I live. 'You are the only one who has gotten my heart, and I will not give it anybody other than you. I could have been engaged many times since you left me. Only God knows that I have not had another boyfriend since you left. You cannot believe how much I love you, my sweetheart, and when I think about how nice you have been to me, then the tears will run from my eyes. If I hear that you have forgotten me, then I will be sure that it will be the end of me, my heart could not take such a blow. Only God knows how long we live, and when we have been loyal to each other, then we have nothing to be sorry for.

Often when I have been ill, I wished that you were here by my side, then I could talk to you, my dear Hans. It is difficult to think back to the first time we came together. I remember how naughty I was toward you. It was not because I did not like you. It was because my love was not truly burning in my heart. But I hope that you have forgiven me all this, and my dear Hans, I beg you to come home again. The ship Beskytteren *is often in Bergen. You cannot believe how glad I would be if you would come home again. The time of waiting is long, but I will wait, and I hope that you will not push my love away from you. Do you know the last evenings we were together? I hope you never will forget what a promise we gave each other.*

There is not so much news. Davine is now healthy. Kristian and Davine are engaged, but there are many who have doubts about her being quite normal. Edward Hansen has gone to Copenhagen to a doctor. Andreas and Johannah are not engaged any more. She is in Torshavn. Andreas sends you greetings and says he wishes for you to come home again. I am going to learn to sew with Alexander Joensen. Now Sunneva has become sick, and I am staying here for a while to take care of the others.

I will now stop writing, and I send my best wishes to my forever beloved friend, and I will never forget you. I wish you a Merry Christmas and a nice New Year. I hope that we will meet each other in the new year. My dear, you have to think about coming home again. Write as soon as possible. The last two letters I got from you were written in August and September. Goodbye and live well.

Maren

LOVE LETTERS

∾

In this letter, Maren mentions for the first time that she and Hans were engaged, though apparently they had never publicly announced it. My father's family seemed to treat her as one of the family. This postcard was included with the above letter.

∾

{Postcard}
To Hans Jacobsen

> *Fuglefjord 16 December 1917*
> *From your sweetheart, Merry Christmas and a Lovely New*
> *Year. Greetings from your loving friend, Maren*

∾

> *Fuglefjord, 20 January 1918*

My Beloved Friend,
Now in this quiet silent afternoon I will write to you, my beloved friend. It is Sunday, and all the young people have gone to a dance, but for me it is better when my thoughts are with you, my beloved friend. I am not real good tonight, because I did not get any letter from you. I thought that I would get a letter from you, and I was very sad that I did not get any. It is the third letter that I have written to you since I got any from you. I can only hope that you have not forgotten me. My dear Hans, now two years have passed since we said to each other that it should be us two. I always thought that there was a big love between us. Now it seems to be blown out. I cannot believe it. I cannot take it. And I always think that it is not so. I have nothing bad to say about you. I have always thought that you loved me, and I hope that you will not now forget me. We have said to each other that we have given our hearts to each other and have to be loyal toward each other. I will beg the Lord to help us. My love, I really wish to hear from you.

105

My loving friend, you don't know how much I love you and how much I miss you, you who must sail on the sea. It is hard in the winter. Seamen have many discomforts and unpleasant moments.

My friend, there is not much new to tell you. Everything is the same. I was sick since before Christmas, but thanks to God I am healthy again. I have been to the doctor, and he says my heart is better now and he says I will completely recover, and I am very happy about that because I have suffered much from the heart problem.

Edward Hansen has become quite healthy. He went to Copenhagen to see a doctor, and he has become quite healthy. He will come back soon.

My love, now you must remember to write so I don't become sad waiting for the letters and getting nothing when the ship comes. I long so much to hear how you are.

The best wishes from your loving friend who will never in this life forget you. May the Lord hold his hands over you and preserve you wherever you go. May luck and happiness follow you wherever you go.

From

Maren

Today they have gotten a letter from Johannus i Tovuni. He is well.

ᘓ

In front of family and friends Maren always tried to appear confident of Hans' love, but in this letter she expresses her anguish and her doubt that Hans will ever return to her. It was a year and two months before she wrote to him again.

ᘓ

Fuglefjord, 2 April 1919

My Dear Sweetheart,

Thank you for the letter I got from you yesterday. It is a great pleasure that now I can take time to write to you again. I have been very sad for a long time, because I could not write a letter to you. It was a great pleasure for me to get a letter from you, my dear friend, so I can know that you are well where you go. My dear friend, it is now more than a year since you last got a letter from me, and you did not know how I was. I am well, and wish you the same, but I cannot believe that you always are well when you are always traveling on the sea.

My dear sweetheart, I am very happy tonight because I am able to sit here with my thoughts only on you and write to you, my true friend. Only God knows how much I love you with my whole heart, and my life has been so true to you. I believe no other girl would have lived as I do. Dear, I will never forget you as long as the blood is warm in my body. You cannot believe how much I am thinking about you, you are in my thoughts night and day. I am longing so much for you. I wish you were here by my side. It is so nice when two who love each other so much, and have lived faithfully for each other, and are able to meet each other without having deceived each other, then it is nice to meet again. I hope that day will come, and we will meet as hopeful as we were when we separated.

My dear friend, there should be some news to tell you, because it has been such a long time since I last wrote.

Joen Pauli Olsen is married to a girl from Sorvag. Axel and Elsebeth Marie are also married. There are not so many new engagements to tell you. Hilda and Andreas Andreasen have each put a ring on their finger to establish the engagement. Sigrid has done the same with a boy from Toftir. All the others are Hans Elias and Malene, Ole Hansen and Maria Hognesen, Hans a Dalbo and Anne Katrine Djurhus, Lene Ore and Joen Midjord, Davine and Kristian Petersen. Now it seems that everything is okay with Davine. Kristian Petersen and Kristian Thomsen have learned to skipper this winter.

Some time ago I spoke with Maks Petersen, and he asked me to send regards from him. He misses you a lot because you two were so often together. Maks has had bad luck. You know Petra and Maks were engaged. Last summer Petra went to Torshavn to work. She had only been there for a short time when she took sick and got tuberculosis. She went to the hospital, and we hoped that she could be well again. She had only been in the hospital for three months when the Lord called her home. Maks had lived a nice life with her, so he has nothing to repent. We are not very safe here on the earth, and we do not know when the Lord may call us home, even if we are in the prime of our youth. But if we have lived here on earth as He wills, then we have nothing to be sorry about.

My dear Hans, I often pray for you, and I wish that He will hear me and bring you back to me. I hope you will come back, and that it will be soon.

THE MISSING SON — A FAROE ISLAND SAGA

I am not tired of waiting because you are the best for me. There is nobody in this world that I have more love for than you. I have given you my heart. Yes I really love you and I believe that you also love me. You have been very kind to me, the first time we were together I did not deserve it, but that we will forget.

My dear friend, I cannot write more tonight because I have so much sewing to do for Easter. I often have to use the nights also, even if I am sewing all day long. Next week I go to Andefjord to sew, and then I will come back and then we will have confirmation here.

I am sending you a photo of me that I just got. I was on a trip to Torshavn and I had a photo taken. I was not dressed so well, but I will send you a better one later. I am sad that I have no picture of you so I can see your smiling face. It is nearly 2 ½ years since we saw each other. I think that I will not know your picture. Maybe you will say the same when you see my picture. Please send me a photo of you.

Now I must stop for this time, but I will write again soon. At last, kind regards from your own loving friend,

Maren

Excuse the letter, because it was written in a hurry. Write again as soon as possible.

Me and Anna Malene were in the photo together, but I have cut her out because I thought you were not interested in getting a photo of her. Greetings from Andreas Joensen.

જી

I wonder if Maren mentions the engagements of other couples to prod Hans to think of marriage. My father had two photos of Maren with the papers and letters from the Faroe Islands, and my cousins recognized her. In the early part of the twentieth century, tuberculosis was a common disease in the Faroe Islands, and I knew of several neighbors and friends who had been hospitalized in the tuberculosis sanitarium in Tórshavn.

જી

(not dated – probably April or May 1919)

My Beloved Friend,

Now I will start again to write for now. I have to tell you something new. You have not heard from me for a long time.

You will smile when you read this. Albert's Sigrid is married and her husband is from Toftir. Andreas and Hildur are going to marry next autumn. They built their house there.

Hans and Thomas from Toftir, you know who they are dating. There are not so many new engagements – Anna Malene Eliason and a boy from Toftir, the farmer's Malene and Hans Elias, Tronde's Hannu and a Danish man, Anna Katrina Djurhus and someone from Gøta.

And now comes the funniest part. The farmer's Bergithe and an English skipper. I think they are engaged. He was here just before the war started. He was with a trawler that was anchored off of the beach (I don't know if you remember it). They got engaged then. Two years ago he was here and he also visited her then. This autumn he started to sail to the Faroe Islands again. He started to visit the farmer's house in full dress uniform. The farmer's house is so small that it is not big enough for him, so they are staying with Andreas. There are parties every time he is here, and you can imagine that we are having great fun.

You should have been here at Christmas. At that time we had a party and the farmer was there. He was very proud that Bergithe is engaged to a rich skipper. When he arrives, he blows the whistle on the boat, and when he comes to the beach he almost sails up to the farmer's door. If he had a small bridge he could walk in. And you should hear when we speak English. You would laugh at us. Johannus i Tovuni is sailing with the same boat. It has been five years since he was here. You can't believe how happy they are to see him again. They are at home now. They are coming back again next week, and she will get some jewelry. She thinks she is very fine.

Jacob Haraldsen has married the daughter of Ole the farmer in Lervig. They had a big wedding. There were many people from here, and it was very fun. Maks sends you greetings. His girlfriend is dead. I think I wrote that before. He is not engaged. Andreas Joensen also sends you greetings and says he wishes you were here and having a party with us. Next Sunday we will have a dancing party.

Now I don't know more to write tonight. I will write again soon. Please write to me, and if you are busy I would appreciate just a few lines. Please send me some postcards from the places you have been, and some Norwegian songs, if you can get them. I have nothing to send you tonight. Next time I will send something. Now I will end these lines with friendly and loving greetings from your sweetheart.

Maren
Write soon and live well.
Jacob Martin also sends you greetings.

∽

In the Faroe Islands, the title "Farmer" is one of respect, which is passed on from father to eldest son. In many towns, the Farmer held property in trust for the government, and served as a local representative for visiting dignitaries. Often, the Farmer was the most prosperous person in the town. When I met the Farmer's Wife in Kirkjubøur, she said that her husband was the 16th Farmer in continuous line since the 1500's.

∽

Fuglefjord, 9 June 1919

My Beloved Friend,
It is a great pleasure for me to write to you again. I have not been well in the past days, but now I am better. When I caught cold, I also got pneumonia. The first time I was very bad off, and then it got better and better. It has now been three weeks since I caught cold. I have been out of bed now for 4 days, and now it seems that I am well.

When I was ill, my old love, Poul from Andefjord, came and visited me. He has now been sailing for two years with a ship from Klaksvik. They are sailing to Spain and other countries. I asked him to forgive me, and that I was glad that we did not hate each other any more. Poul is a good person, and I wish him all the best. He is now engaged to someone in Klaksvik. I have a beautiful photo of him. Of you I do not have any yet. It seems that is strange. I do not believe that you are always so busy that you cannot get a photo taken.
....

LOVE LETTERS

⚬

Apparently some pages were lost from this letter. In several letters Maren mentioned Poul from Andefjord, and here she notes that he is her old love, from the time before she and Hans were together. The fact that she didn't have a photo of Hans was a constant annoyance to Maren and made her doubt his commitment to her. Instead, she has a photo of her old love.

Maren continued to write to Hans for several more years, but the letters became more sporadic, and sometimes there were long gaps between letters, and the mood of her letters fluctuated between hope and despair.

OVERLEAF: This is the main street where it enters Fuglafjørður, and snow-covered Mount Blábjørg towers over the town. ➤

Fuglafjørður, December 2008: During the past few days, I have been learning to walk all over again. When I first learned to walk, quite a few years ago, I am quite sure that the ground didn't deliberately try to knock me down, like it is doing now. I have lived in the San Francisco Bay Area all of my life, and we don't have snow. I do not know how people are able to walk on slippery, icy, snowy, wet streets. This time of year, there are a lot of Christmas events in the Faroe Islands, and if I want to participate, I need to learn to walk in the snow, at least up the hill to my car.

Sunday afternoon at 4:30 was the tree-lighting ceremony in Fuglafjørður. I put on my snow boots, two coats and several scarves and drove up to the town. I arrived right on time, and I think I was about the third person to arrive. I found a quiet place to stand near the library, almost out of the wind, where I could see the tall Christmas tree on the hill above me. Within half an hour, several hundred people arrived, filling the street, sidewalks, and parking lots. Children were running and playing in the snow, sliding down the pathway from the library, turning it into a smooth, icy slope.

Then the brass band arrived and started setting up their music stands all around me. I was not in a quiet place out of the wind, but instead I was center-stage. I knew that if I tried to walk down the icy pathway (or even worse, the icy stairs) the ice would do its best to knock me over, while several hundred people watched. Instead I eased my way carefully into the shrubbery a little behind the band. Once again, I selected the wrong place, because some other people arrived and set up the microphone right next to me. I retreated a little further into the shrubbery, trying not to damage the snow-covered plants, and pretended to be fascinated by the speeches in Faroese. It was cold, dark, windy, and wet, but everyone had a wonderful time. After the band played, the Christmas tree lights were turned on. Then everyone walked through the slushy snow across the street to the Culture House for hot chocolate and sweet rolls. I walked very slowly and carefully on the steep, icy streets, while everyone else seemed to breeze right on past me.

Monday evening, I put on coats, scarves, and boots again and went to choir rehearsal. It had been snowing off and on all day, thawing and refreezing the snow into sheets of ice. My street had a layer of ice, topped with a few inches of snow, with an inch or two of rainwater and melted snow running through

CELEBRATION AND FAREWELL

it. I could walk as long as I held onto the fence, but at the end of the fence, I had to turn around and return home. Then I remembered the pair of ice-crampons someone had given me as a gift. They worked! I walked carefully up to my car, drove very slowly up the hills to the school, and walked down the long, steep driveway and across the tile patio through the icy snow. Quite an accomplishment! Of course, some people do this every day during the winter, but remember that I am just learning to walk.

Chapter 8 – Celebration and Farewell

Saturday morning the whole town of Fuglafjørður was filled with a buzz of activity. This was the opening day of the Varmakelda (**VARM**ah**CHELD**ah) festival. Early in the morning large trucks carefully maneuvered their way along the narrow side streets, turning the sharp corner in front of Poul Jacob's house and heading down the steep hill toward the harbor, bringing boats from all over the islands for the races that were to be held in the bay in the afternoon. The trucks had to use the narrow side streets because the main street into town was blocked with carnival booths and food concessions.

After a late breakfast we walked down to the main street for the opening ceremonies which included music, speeches, and a crowd of people. The brass band, with of members of all ages, played several numbers. Children and young people from all of the sports teams lined up wearing their team uniforms. Jógvan Árge gave the opening address, and while he was talking, my cousins said to me, "He's talking about you." Later, Mr. Árge gave me a copy of his introductory remarks, both in Faroese and English.

Varmakelda 1997

Fuglafirðingar (people from Fuglafjørð) around the world – unite. This could be the headline for this year's Varmakelda, because it must be a very

THE MISSING SON — A FAROE ISLAND SAGA

rare experience that a village, the same week as the annual festival is arranged, is host to visitors from the other side of the world – people searching for their roots.

It is also very rare that men and women, well beyond their prime, suddenly receive the news that they have two living cousins way over in San Francisco – cousins they had no knowledge of whatsoever.

This is almost the story about the return of the prodigal son! And returned he has – Hans Jacobsen, whom none of the relatives "i Lon" in Fuglafjørð had heard of or seen at all since 1924.

The general thought has been that he was lost at sea in the twenties or during the War, but the simple reality was that they only lost connection when he went ashore in America, and now his daughter has seen to it that the connection is re-established.

You may wonder if Hans i Lon forgot about the Faroes. Maybe he did, but blood runs thicker than water, so he kept the Faroes. And the fact that he didn't throw the Faroes away is the reason that the connection has been re-established.

Had this mysterious sailor from Fuglafirði not been so careful with his memories about the Faroes and if he hadn't kept every letter from home and every paper from his voyages around the world early in this century, there would be no connection today.

And his descendants in California would not have had many chances of finding the roots that are so important to all people, and his daughter Jennifer Henke, who is present here today, would never have found out where the cradle stood.

Over and over again I heard how important it was that I had come to the Faroe Islands, not just for my family, but for all people in the Faroes. They welcomed me as though I had returned home after being gone for a long, long time. My perspective was a little different. I felt like I had finally found a place that had only existed only in my imagination.

In the afternoon I walked down to the harbor to watch the boat races. The docks were packed solidly with people, all of them in a holiday mood. No one was bothered by the misty rain. Dozens of boats were maneuvered down the steep ramp into the water. Each boat

CELEBRATION AND FAREWELL

had eight or ten rowers, and the early races were with younger athletes, beginning with boys and girls about 10 to 12 years and finishing with teams of men in their twenties. The boats for each race would make their way out to the starting point a kilometer or two away by circling around the far edge of the bay. The finish line was a row of buoys stretched most of the way across the bay. Cars lined the road leading into town, where people parked to watch the races. Jógvan Árge announced the races from a coast guard boat that accompanied the racers, and his voice was broadcast over the whole harbor. Each race had six to twelve boats, and the racing lasted most of the afternoon. After the races, all of the boats were loaded back onto the trucks, and it was a long time before the last truck had rumbled out of town.

After dinner I walked up to the high school playing field to watch a soccer game. There were no seats or bleachers, but the crowd stood on the street uphill from the playing field in the light rain, and ticket sellers collected our money before we could enter the street. By this time, I was getting a little tired of standing outside in the rain

Sunday morning I slept late and didn't go to church with Poul Jacob and Jutta. In the afternoon we went down to the main street for the closing ceremonies of the festival. After spending a week in the town, I seemed to know a lot of people – many of them relatives. One elderly man said he remembered my father, though he would have been about four years old when my father left the Faroes. A small orchestra accompanied folk dancers from Denmark and Norway. The ceremony ended with everyone joining in singing of Faroese ballads, linking arms to dance the chain dance. By the time they finished, there were a hundred people and more, young and old, singing and dancing in the town square. They didn't sing all of the ballads, thankfully. There are well over 70,000 verses. Before the Faroes had a written language, history and legends were recorded in ballads, and every year at the national festivals people were reminded of their country's past by song and dance. It was a time when the people of all ages came together, including my cousins in their 70's and 80's along with their great grandchildren as young as 6 or 7 years.

Many people were dressed in the traditional native dress. The men wore dark blue woven woolen knee length breeches and long sleeved woolen jackets with silver buttons down both sides of the front, bright

119

woolen vests with more silver buttons, long woolen stockings, and silver buckles on black shoes. The women wore dresses with long full skirts, a contrasting laced bodice with silver buttons, and a long elaborately embroidered apron over the skirt, with a matching triangular shawl over the shoulders, fastened in front with a silver brooch. Many of the clothes echoed the colors of the flag, red, white, and blue, but the outfits were all different, with materials of different patterns and textures.

In the evening we went to Lillian and Bernhard's home, and after dinner an editor and photographer from one of the Tórshavn newspapers arrived to interview me and hear my story firsthand. I showed him the letters from my father's family, the old photographs, and sailing records. He planned to do a feature story for the following Saturday edition of the paper. Four of my cousins came so we could be photographed together. I didn't see the article until a year later on my next visit to the Faroes. Half of the front page was a photo of me with my cousin Martin, who resembles my father, and the headline was "Cousin from America." The story inside covered about 4 pages and included many of the photographs that I brought with me.

Later in the evening we walked to one of the factory cafeterias, which had been turned into a coffee house and performance hall for the weekend. The room was crowded with people, both performers and audience, and many of them were my relatives. I was amazed to find so much musical talent from a town of 1500 people. Several people commented to me that the Jacobsen family from Fuglafjørður has many talented musicians.

On Monday I realized that my time in the Faroes was nearly over, with only two days left. There was one sight-seeing trip that I still wanted to take – a boat trip to the Vestmanna Bird Cliffs on the north west coast of Streymoy – but the weather had been stormy for several days and the boats had been unable to make the trip. By Monday afternoon, the storms had subsided enough that an afternoon trip was scheduled, and Bernhard agreed to take me. The small boat leaving Vestmanna was quite crowded with about 25 passengers, but I found a place to stand where I had a good view and a chance to take photos of the scenery. The boat left the calm waters of the Vestmanna harbor

Cousins in Fuglafjørður, from left, Petra Hentze, Diana Lundsbjerg, Jennifer Henke, Poul Jacob Hansen, and Martin Jacobsen.

and headed north toward the open ocean, where the water was very choppy and the waves crashed continuously on the shore. Within a few minutes, we could see the cliffs ahead. The temperature on the boat dropped as we left the seclusion of the harbor, and strong winds from the northwest blew over and through us. I was glad I was wearing two pairs of wool socks, two pairs of pants, and two wool sweaters under my coat. I didn't have any mittens, so I pulled my sweater sleeves over my hands. Coming from the San Francisco Bay area, with its moderate year-round climate, I didn't even own many warm clothes, but at least I had my new warm Faroese wool sweater.

The tour-boat operator gave a running commentary and told many stories, which Bernhard translated for me. High above us on the upper slopes of the cliffs we could see sheep grazing and barbed-wire fences separating sections of land. Every spring the sheep are brought out by boat and then raised by ropes to the fields on the tops of the cliffs. The farmers know exactly how many sheep each section will support, 25 in this section, 40 in the next, and so forth. Then in October they must go out with the boats again and bring the sheep down from the cliffs for the winter to the safety of barns and fields near the towns

I found the wild landscape fascinating. Creeks from the high hills above had carved deep crevasses in the rock, and the water rushed and tumbled down the hillsides or dropped over the cliffs in spectacular waterfalls. The wind and water had carved the rocky cliffs, and we passed rounded spiral sea stacks and sharp needle-like spires rising hundreds of feet above us. Sea caves and tunnels had been created by the strong currents. Normally the tour boats sail through some of these tunnels, but we weren't able to because of the rough weather. We did sail through a narrow passage with high cliffs on one side and a row of sea stacks rising above us on the other.

Then, of course, there were the birds, countless birds, nesting on every ledge and crevasse on the cliffs above us, thousands and millions of birds of dozens of different species. Some birds were still incubating their eggs, and some eggs had already hatched. Bernhard pointed out the guillemot, which is black with a white chest. When the birds are incubating their eggs, they sit facing the cliffs, holding the eggs on their feet to prevent them from falling off the cliff. After the eggs have hatched, the birds sit facing the ocean. We could see the black backs of some of these birds that were still waiting for their eggs to hatch, and for others we could see the white fronts. Early July is still the height of the nesting season. Many species of birds migrate north in the summer, and the Faroe Islands are prime breeding grounds. Then in the late summer and early fall, the birds leave the Faroe Islands for warmer weather in the south. The Faroe Islands are the breeding grounds for 68 different species of birds, and 225 different species have been found there.

After spending 2½ hours on the boat being blown by north Atlantic winds, sprayed by salty ocean waves, and rinsed by the misty rain, I was hoping to go home, dry my hair, and change into dry clothes. Instead we stopped for dinner in Gøta with Esmann's family.

Sharp rock spire rises from the ocean along the Vestmanna bird cliffs. Our boat sailed between the cliffs and a row of tall sheer sea stacks, with birds nesting on every ridge and crevasse.

THE MISSING SON — A FAROE ISLAND SAGA

After dinner we went to see the church in Gøta, where Esmann was the organist. The most striking feature of this church is the stained glass window behind the altar, created by a Faroese artist Tróndur Patursson, the twin brother of the Farmer from Kirkjubøur, where I had been a few days earlier. The window depicts Jesus ascending to heaven, looking down on a boat swamped by waves and the disciples on the shore looking up at Jesus. There were many additional items made of stained glass, including the pulpit, the lighting fixtures, the baptismal font, the communion rail, glasses, and plates – all made by the same artist. We were very late getting home after a very long day.

On Tuesday, my last day in the Faroes, Poul Jacob took me to see the northern islands, six islands in the north east part of the Faroes. First we took the ferry from Lervík to Klaksvík on the island of Borðoy, then we drove north to the end of the road. I think the road from Klaksvík to Víðareiði may be the scariest stretch of road in the Faroe Islands. I was still getting used to driving on the narrow, one lane roads, with turnouts to use when we met a car coming toward us. The steep cliffs above us didn't bother me nearly as much as the cliffs and steep slopes going down to the ocean on the other side. However the scariest part of all were the two tunnels on Borðoy, each of them several kilometers long, without lights, and one narrow lane with periodic turnouts and a deep ditch on each side to carry away the rain-water. I preferred the cliffs and the ocean in the daylight to the pitch black one-lane tunnel with deep ditches on both sides with bright headlights coming toward us in the dark.

We crossed from Borðoy to Viðoy on a short causeway, and then drove on a narrow one-lane road along the edge of a cliff to the northern end of the island. We stopped for lunch at a large resort hotel in Viðareiði (pronounced *vWEEahoyih*), where we were served a tray of open-faced sandwiches, each one a work of art. We were the only people in the large dining hall. I admired the jagged mountains to the north of the town, but it wasn't until later that I realized that these were the tops of sheer cliffs, with nothing beyond them but ocean. These cliffs include the Enniberg promontory, the most northern part of the Faroes and Europe's highest promontory, with a sheer drop to the ocean of

CELEBRATION AND FAREWELL

2300 feet. To the east we could see the islands of Fugloy and Svínoy, which can be reached by catching a ride on the mail boat.

Tuesday night Poul Jacob's whole family came for a farewell dinner, and everyone had gifts for me. After dinner, relatives dropped by in a steady stream to tell me good-bye and bring me gifts. I felt overwhelmed with their kindness, generosity, and genuine affection. I also felt overwhelmed at the prospect of trying to get everything into my already bulging suitcases. I was grateful for suitcases with expandable zippered panels. I was also very thankful to Gurið's husband, Dan, for repairing my broken suitcase, which now could stand upright. It was well after midnight when I said my last farewells and closed the last zipper on my suitcases. It seemed incredible that I had been in the Faroe Islands only two weeks. So much had happened in such a short time. I lay in bed wondering how I could remember the strong emotions that my visit had evoked. I stayed up most of the night (what was left of it), writing a poem about my father's homeland and the islands that captured my heart.

Wednesday morning Poul Jacob and Bernhard drove me to the airport. When we arrived, everything was fogged in, and Mærsk passengers from Monday and Tuesday were still waiting for their flight to Copenhagen. Bernhard and Poul Jacob waited with me for a few hours, but finally they left to go home. Mid-afternoon, busses arrived to take us to the nearby hotel for a hot meal, provided by the airlines. The large hotel dining room appeared to be designed to accommodate airline passengers delayed by foggy weather. Long tables stretched across the room from wall to wall, and the meal was served family style, with large platters and bowls of food placed at regular intervals. I walked back to the airport in the light rain rather than waiting for the crowded bus. As I approached the airport, I could hear an airplane coming in, through the clouds, for a landing. It was a small airplane from the Faroese airline Atlantic Air, which was able to land under the cloud cover. The larger Mærsk airplane was unable to land and had already returned to Copenhagen.

All announcements in the airport were made in four languages, just as they had been on my flight to the Faroes. English was always last, and by the time they got to the English announcements, the crowded

125

airport was so noisy that I couldn't understand what was being said, especially since the English had a strong Faroese accent. At about 11:00 p.m., the airport started sending people to hotels for the night. I missed the announcements because of the noise, but finally I went to the airport office to find out what was happening. They gave me a ticket for the night for a hotel in Vestmanna, but when I got outside, the bus for Vestmanna was gone. I mistakenly got on the local bus which was taking people to Sørvágar for bed and breakfast hosted by residents of the town, and the bus driver was able to find a home with an extra room for me. The small house had a kitchen and sitting room on the lower level, and very steep stairs, nearly a ladder, led to the upper floor, which had two small bedrooms and a bathroom. My room wasn't too clean, the wood was old and rotting in the corners, but it looked much better than the crowded airport. The supports on the beds were sagging so much that the beds were more like hammocks, so I took the mats off of both beds and stacked them in the middle of the floor. The room was stifling hot, but I finally figured out how to turn down the steam heater in the corner. In spite of everything, I slept very well.

The next morning the cloud cover was high, and I had hopes that the plane would be able to land without difficulty, but by the time it arrived from Copenhagen, the clouds were so low that the plane was diverted to Norway, instead. During breakfast, the woman who owned the home told me that she recognized me from the television interview. Later, while I was waiting in the airport again, I was surprised to see several relatives. Sigvør brought her parents, Esmann and Gunnleyg, who were on their way to Sweden for a holiday, and their son Joan Pauli was on his way to Iceland to join his fishing ship.

When the Mærsk plane finally landed at 11:30, the whole airport erupted with shouting and cheering. It sounded like a soccer game. Passengers from Monday and Tuesday had priority on the flight, but my relatives were looking out for me and made sure I was the first passenger from Wednesday's flight to get a boarding pass.

I had wished that I could extend my visit in the Faroe Islands, but I should have been more specific in my wish. I really didn't want to spend my extra time at the airport.

AN ABLE-BODIED SEAMAN

*OVERLEAF: Hans Jacobsen made several trips to the
Far East with the S/S Bearport in 1922-23.* ➤

THE MISSING SON — A FAROE ISLAND SAGA

Airports, October 2008: *Between Friday morning Pacific time and Saturday night Greenwich time, I spent approximately eleven hours in various airports. It seems that, involuntarily, I am becoming an expert at waiting. There are a number of ways to pass the time while waiting in an airport, and here are some of the things I tried this past weekend: made a phone call, read a book, knitted, read a foreign language newspaper very slowly, talked for an hour to a stranger (who operates a hotel in Iceland), and slept. By the end of the day on Saturday, this last one was becoming predominant. However, I think my all-time favorite airport activity is people-watching.*

I wonder how much you can tell about a culture by watching people in airports. I suspect it is quite a lot.

Airport number one was in San Francisco. Everything proceeded on schedule until our plane pulled away from the terminal to taxi out to the runway, where we joined a queue of 20-30 planes waiting for takeoff. This was San Francisco's Fleet Week, and the Navy's Blue Angel fighter jets were using the airport to prepare for the air show over the San Francisco Bay on Saturday. While we were waiting, I watched as four jets lined up across the adjacent runway, wing-tip to wing-tip, accelerated down the runway side by side, and thundered off over the bay in a cloud of smoke. As a result, we were an hour late leaving SF, but we arrived in Chicago only thirty minutes late.

Some of the thoughts that came to my mind in the San Francisco Airport were:

- *Don't talk to strangers unless absolutely necessary.*
- *Hurry or get out of the way.*
- *Keep your eyes on your luggage except to check your watch.*

My overall impression was that people were traveling in a polite isolation.

Airport number two was Chicago/O'Hare, where I had to make my way from one edge of the domestic airport to the far side of the international terminal. However, I had an hour and a half, which seemed like a lot of time.

Direction signs in this airport are not only confusing, but contradictory. I followed several signs and arrows toward terminal 5 (going west, I think). Then the signs disappeared, so I stopped and looked all around me for more signs. I saw signs for terminal 5 behind me, so I turned around and headed back east, as several signs directed. Then the signs disappeared again, so I stopped again, changed direction again, and followed the signs pointing west again. This could have gone on for a long time. I even stopped under one sign and carefully looked at both sides, and each side had an arrow pointing straight ahead to terminal 5, one pointing east and one west. I changed my tactic and decided ask for directions, walk a couple hundred feet, and ask directions again. Most often, when I asked how to get to the international terminal, the response was, "Oh, that's a long ways away." By the time I found the international terminal, went through another security check-point and down long corridors to my gate, they were already starting to load the plane.

This waiting room had a very different feel from the one in San Francisco. This was a Scandinavian Air flight with a destination of Copenhagen, and all around me people were conversing in Danish.

Chapter 9 – An Able-bodied Seaman

My father sailed full time for about 14 years, from age 15 through 29. I knew that he had traveled around much of the world, but it was difficult for me to find out much information from his sailing days. I remember only a few things he told me when I was a child. For him, "The War" was World War I, when he was sailing and seeing the effects of war first hand. I remember he said he was on a ship that sailed to India during the war, and as a white man, he did not get off the ship, because the Indian people had such hatred for Germans that they would shoot a white person on sight, and ask questions later. I also remember he said he had been through the Suez and Panama Canals.

After I married, my husband Curt was able to get my father to talk about his sailing days, and we began making a recording of some of my father's sailing stories. Whenever we visited my parents we would add a little more to the tape. Unfortunately, this was interrupted when my husband was drafted into the military a few months later, but we did tape about 30 minutes of stories. My father was 73 years old at the time of these recordings.

Among the papers that my father saved were his sailing records and photographs of ships he sailed on. The papers included ship discharge papers, pay records, letters of recommendation, sailors' union records, and so forth. Many of these were in Norwegian from the Norwegian ships he was with, and my cousins in the Faroe Islands translated

133

them for me. The three letters he wrote to his parents that were saved also include some information about his travels, and he also saved a few envelopes from his family, addressed to him in different parts of the world.

When my father was growing up, schooling in the Faroe Islands went only to the seventh or eighth grade. Like many young men, my father started sailing full time when he finished school in about 1911, but even before that, he spent much of his time at sea.

When I was nine or ten years or so, I spent more time on the boat than I did at home. One night we came home at about midnight. We had quite a ways to travel, about 30 miles to come home. It was a beautiful summer night. And all of a sudden something happened. Something jumped out of the water and we saw it coming down. It was just like a building falling down. It was a big whale. It kind of scared us for a while, and it was a while before we got over it. We had seen them before, but not in that part of the islands. We were in between two islands, and we had never seen big whales come in there before. History said that only one whale had come through there before. The whales were kind of scared to come in there between the islands because there were awfully strong currents. They had to fight their way in and they had to know which way the current was going so the current would help them coming and going.

When my father started sailing full time, he sailed primarily in the waters around the Faroes and later he sailed to Iceland, Norway, Denmark, England, and Northern Europe. Here are some of his comments about his early years of sailing and fishing near Iceland.

Sometimes we would see pilot whales very close. You could almost reach them sometimes, with your hand. They would float around near the ship. When you climb up in the rigging, especially around Iceland, there were lots of porpoises. You could see them for miles. You could climb up in the rigging and look all around the ocean and you could see porpoises just jumping up and down continuously. They never collided with one another. They came very close, but didn't collide. They are almost like sheep. When you get a herd of sheep together they rub against each other, but they never hurt each other. Well, we couldn't see them in the water, but when they come out of the water they just barely miss each other.

AN ABLE-BODIED SEAMAN

A few times we tried eating porpoises. One time crossing the Atlantic there was a big Finlander who had been on whaling boats. One time he got a notion to get a harpoon – a hand-harpoon. You put them into the whales or porpoises and then you can pull them up, and he did this a couple of times. You can throw the harpoon hard enough just with your arms. The boats are not too high, you are down close to the water, and they come right close to the boat, just barely an inch or two away when they follow the boats. Some of them take a notion and they can follow you for miles. You know on the boats there is always a man at night, a lookout they call it, looking out for other ships, and if he sees anything dangerous or unusual he will report it to the officers. In his spare time he could watch the porpoises going by. It was really interesting. If they want to get away from the boat they can, and then you just don't see them any more, but most of the time they just follow the boat. There were porpoises pretty much everywhere.

We didn't see sharks so often. We saw one up around Iceland. You could catch them on a line. Out at sea there is deep sea fishing, about 600 feet or so. We used the measure of a fathom, a hundred fathoms or so of water, and when they are down there that deep they are not wild. You just feel a little nibble once in a while or just a little shake. If you do surface fishing here you would have a whole day's job just getting it in. I got one, one time. It was about 14 feet long, and we cut the liver out of it and threw the rest away. We got a good price for the liver. There are so many different types of sharks. They have two rows – two sets of teeth. On the big ships, you don't have any trouble with sharks. It has been heard that they have on small boats. On the small boats sometimes they bother them, but not often.

In November 1916, Hans took a job as a sailor on a schooner sailing from Tórshavn and during the next several years he sailed primarily in the North Atlantic. In May 1919 he signed with the Norwegian ship, the *S/S Otta*, and made his first trip to America, sailing to Vancouver and other Pacific ports. In 1921, the ship was laid up for repairs in Emden, Germany, and Hans signed with the Canadian ship, the *City of Vancouver*, which was sailing from Emden to Vancouver.

I was on a Norwegian ship that paid off at the end in Germany, and the ship tied up there and was laid up for repair, and so everybody left the

135

ship. I got on a Canadian ship that went from Germany up to Vancouver in British Colombia. When we were a couple of days out at sea we found that there were two stowaways on board, but nobody knew it until then. By then they wanted to keep on going. They were going to take them up to British Colombia, but there was a drawback there. The company would have to pay their fare back to Germany, and that part of it they didn't like, and the boys didn't want to go back to Germany either. They made a plan there to escape, and we were helping them along. We were building a raft for them, but the officers didn't know it. It was about 10 feet long by about 8 feet wide. They hung the raft off the stern.

The officers didn't see us building it. They didn't know at that time that we were building it. But then they found out that something was going on and they started investigating. We were going to throw the raft overboard, and the stowaways were going to jump over and get onto it. But the officers thought it was a good idea, and they wanted to get in on it too and help them out. They made a fake repair on the engine and stopped the engine for a while. They had to make a minor repair, or were supposed to. If they stopped the boat they had to enter it in the log book, but they had to leave out the information about the stowaways. The stowaways got on the raft, off the coast of British Colombia, and we didn't know anything about what happened.

But about two years later I was on a Norwegian ship again going from British Colombia down to South America, and we stopped at Mazatlan (Mexico), and there I met one of the men who had been a stowaway there on the boat. He told me the rest of the story. They had an awful time there. The current was taking them out to sea. They were maybe a couple of miles off shore. They just about had it made and they thought it was a sure bet, but they suffered a lot, both of them. One of them was a younger man, about 20, and the other one was about 27 years of age. And the young man couldn't take it. He lost his mind. There were sharks all around them, and sometimes they tried to get them. He jumped overboard, and the sharks tore him up. The man that I met in Mazatlan told us the story. He was working as a stevedore down there. And I guess that is the end of that story. There were evil people there, in Germany, and he tried to get away from them. That was after World War I.

The ship going from Canada to South America was the *S/S Remus* from the Latin American Line of a Norwegian shipping company.

136

Hans was with the *S/S Bearport* of Vancouver for at least two trips to the Far East in 1922 and 1923. He had several photos of this ship and the crew, and on the back of the photo is a handwritten list of the places where this ship stopped, including Honolulu, American Samoa, Kobe, Shanghai, Hong Kong, Swatow, Yokohama, Zamboanga, New Castle, Djakarta, Surabaji, Padang, Singapore, and San Francisco. This next story probably took place on the *S/S Bearport*.

We never sailed around the Cape of Good Hope or Cape Horn. Instead we sailed through the Suez or the Panama Canal. We sailed mostly in the northern hemisphere, but we did go to Australia and India. One cargo we picked up from India was birds and animals. That was in 1923. That was really a circus before it got to the circus. We didn't exactly have trouble, but we weren't entirely free from it, either.

There was one monkey that was a pet monkey, and everybody played with it. One day he took a notion that he wanted to go up in the rigging, so up he went – he just climbed up. Those were the days we had a wireless wire strung between the masts, from one mast to the other. We had an animal trainer from India who was trying to get him down, but nothing doing. The monkey crawled out on the wireless wire going from one mast to the other. The man couldn't go there, but the monkey made out okay. He said, "Come and get me," but nobody dared to. That went on for about twenty four hours, we tried to get him down, but it was about twenty four hours before he came down again. He got hungry and wanted a banana, and so they got him down. But after that he didn't have the freedom he had before. They put him in a cage. That was an enjoyable trip.

There was one other incident. We had some wild animals, tigers and leopards, and they were down in number four hold, at the back end of the boat. That was where they were all stored. One of the sailors went down there, and he was drunk. He fell asleep in front of the cages there. When someone looked in there, one of the tigers was trying to claw him, but he couldn't reach him. He was just out of reach.

Now on this same trip there was a big snake that got loose, got out of the cage. The animal trainer was there, and he went down to take a look around. Now everybody was scared, because the snake was a monster. I'm not exactly sure how long it was, maybe twenty feet or so. The trainer went down and got him right back in the cage. He said that if you know them, and you aren't harming them, then they won't harm you. That's what he told us. But he said if there is any advantage, then they want to take it first. They have some intelligence.

Frank Buck was the one who caught these animals for an animal company. He came home on the ship, he and his wife. They had to bring the animals to a shipping point. They were hunting them all over India, and then getting them ready for shipping. They don't ship one animal at a time – that would be too expensive. It was in Singapore that we picked them up. That was the shipping point.

At that time I was just a sailor, an able-bodied seaman.

Frank Buck (1884-1950) was an American hunter and collector of wild animals, who later documented his adventures in his books and movies. He began travelling the world in 1911, capturing exotic birds and wild animals and bringing them back to zoos and circuses in America. He authored several books documenting his adventures and also made and starred in a number of adventure movies, featuring wild animals. During his lifetime he brought back alive more than 500 different species of animals and more than 100,000 wild birds.

In 1923 and 1924, Hans served on the *S/S Ventura*, a passenger ship sailing between San Francisco and Sydney, the only passenger ship he served on. He wrote to his parents on 5 July 1923, that he was sailing from San Francisco to Honolulu, on a ship headed for Sydney, and he was Quartermaster, meaning his job was to steer the ship.

I was a boatswain for quite a while, and a quartermaster. That's steering the boat. That was a clean job. No one bothers you – it's sort of a status job. At that time you had to stand two hours at the wheel steering the boat, and two hours on the bridge as a lookout for the officer, so he could have a little time off checking navigation. Four hours at a time, and then you get eight hours off, and four on again. That was a good job. On fishing ships it was four on and four off, and sometimes you had to work twenty four hours without any sleep when fishing was good. But here it didn't make any difference what was going on, you got your four hours work and eight hours off. This was a passenger ship. You have generally better conditions on board passenger ships. This ship was

AN ABLE-BODIED SEAMAN

not a big one, probably about 500 passengers. We didn't have much chance to talk to the passengers. We usually stayed away from them. They were not our class. There were probably over a hundred crewmen all together.

When you were steering the ship, you didn't have to navigate. Someone else did that, and they just told you what compass bearing to take, and you followed it. And you better be good at it, or they will tell you the second time. Sometimes there's a problem in steering the ship the way you wanted to go, and some of the officers don't know it.

We were in Norway, where you have to go in between the rocks. You're not out in the open ocean, and you've got to change course every few minutes to miss the islands. There was a friend of mine who was steering the boat, and the captain didn't like his steering. And so the captain took the wheel, and he almost ran her aground. It was really their fault. When the ship is loaded, if you get her too much on the head, that is too much forward and too deep, it is almost impossible to steer the ship because too much of the rudder is out of the water, and that is what controls it. The captain should know that too, but he thought that he was a better helmsman than the able-bodied seaman. He missed the rocks, all right. He didn't go on shore, but he knew better from then on that what a good helmsman couldn't do, he couldn't do either.

What makes the ship go down in front is the skewing of the cargo. If there is too much weight in the front of the boat, the front goes down. When you unload the ship, you may need to take all of the back section of the cargo out of the boat, and then you go to another port with the rest of the cargo, and by that time it's on its head too much, and that's what happened. And where the current runs strong, it's awfully hard to steer a boat.

Let me tell you one more story from Japan. We were going from Yokohama up to Nagasaki. And it was a rough night. I was at the wheel, and we had a pilot — a Japanese pilot. I can tell you it was hard steering, because the current was turning the boat around, turning it from one side to the other. I was at the wheel, steering the boat. This Japanese pilot was a sun worshipper, and it was just at sunrise. He was lying over on one side of the bridge, and didn't care about the boat. He was praying to the sun, or whatever he was doing. He neglected his duties, but nothing happened. It was just rough going for a while until he came to. He just left his post. Maybe his praying did some good.

Hans Jacobsen, in 1923, is wearing his quartermaster uniform.

AN ABLE-BODIED SEAMAN

Hans told another story about stowaways from his time on the *S/S Ventura* in 1923 or 1924. We have a photo of a ship called the *Sonora*, with a note on the back saying it is a sister ship to the *Ventura*.

There was another stowaway on a passenger boat running between here (San Francisco) and Australia. We left Honolulu and were going south, and there was a sister ship from the same company coming up from Australia. They stopped at American Samoa, and when they were a day or two out at sea again, they found that they had a stowaway. We were going to American Samoa, and they had just left American Samoa coming up north. So the ships got in contact one with the other, and they had to pinpoint the location right out in the middle of the ocean, and they transferred that stowaway onto our boat, and we took him back where he came from. They sent him over to our ship from the other ship, and we took him back again. The poor guy didn't get very far.

On a long stretch like that, you have to navigate pretty closely. You could see other ships straight ahead. It was pretty clear — say two to four miles visibility. You see other ships pretty often. They have what they call shipping lanes. There are some lanes going south from Honolulu by the Philippines, and so forth. They are just about on the same course all the time, traveling the same lane, otherwise they would get to some other islands. There is a danger of colliding with another ship, and it happens occasionally, too.

The longest time I was at sea without coming to land was when we were out fishing. It was three months probably, without setting foot on land. You have to learn to walk again. On a big boat it isn't so bad, but on a smaller ship they rock so fast, you always have to have one long leg and one short leg.

My father was with the *Calebra* from San Francisco in 1924 and 1925, and this is the last ship mentioned in his sailing records. During the following years he worked in the shipyards in San Francisco, and in 1933 he began working for an iron and steel company in San Francisco.

OVERLEAF: Tindholmur is an island/rock between the islands of Vágar and Mykines. ➤

More Airports, October 2008: My next airport was Copenhagen's Kastrup airport. This is a major transfer point for Europe, Africa, Asia, and the West, and I was surrounded by a bedlam of different languages. Once again, I was relieved that the rest of the world has learned English, since my fluency in any foreign language is very limited. Here I had to pick up my checked luggage, take it through terminal 3 to terminal 2, and re-check my bags on Atlantic Air. I have travelled this route enough that this step is fairly routine, and I was hoping for a chance to charge my Faroese cell phone and nap during my 5½ hour stay in Copenhagen. While checking in for this last leg of my flight I heard the bad news first. My flight, due to leave at 7:00 p.m., was delayed until 11:00 p.m. The good news soon followed. The flight from 8:35 in the morning had not left yet, it should be leaving in a couple of hours, and they had room for me. The Faroe Island Airport, where I was headed, had been closed for most of the past two days because of fierce storms, but the weather had cleared, and three of the delayed planes were en route to Copenhagen from the Faroes, and would immediately turn around and fly back to the Faroes with a load of passengers.

I got a revised boarding pass, and went upstairs to go through another security check-point. I'm getting quite good at security check-points. Get 3-4 plastic trays, remove shoes, remove coat, remove plastic bag with liquids, and put these items plus purse in plastic trays. Open suitcase, remove computer, remove CPAP breathing machine, put these items each into their own trays, close suitcase and put it on the moving belt. Then go through security, wait for security personnel to run a test on the CPAP machine, and finally try to put everything back together and zip the suitcase. However, this step had a little glitch. The security guard who checked my passport and boarding pass saw that my plane left at 8:35 in the morning, some six or seven hours earlier, and he didn't think I should be allowed in the boarding area to wait for a plane that had already left. He didn't seem to believe me when I said the plane was delayed. After everyone in the long line had gone through security, he asked one of his co-workers about the flight, and they waved me in. I picked the wrong line that time.

The waiting area of the Copenhagen Airport has more shops and stores than the entire country of the Faroe Islands, and with the high tax rate on commodities in that part of the world, tax-free airport shopping is very popular. I found a comfortable seat in the middle the shops near Terminal A, and prepared

RETURNING TO THE FÆROE ISLANDS

to ignore the bedlam around me. After an hour's wait, they finally posted the gate number for my Atlantic Air flight to the Faroe Islands.

Gates 7, 9, and 11 in terminal A were like a different world. These were the gates used that afternoon for the three daily flights from Copenhagen to the Faroes, the 8:35 a.m., the 12:35 p.m., and the 7:00 p.m. flights. I have often joked that in the Faroe Islands everyone knows everyone else, and when you are in an airport waiting room waiting for a flight to the Faroes, it certainly seems to be true. People were talking, laughing, and moving about the room to talk with their friends. Except for the luggage piled everywhere, it could have been a noisy birthday party or a church social. Since I am only half Faroese, I didn't know everyone, but I did know three passengers. When I entered the waiting room there were only a few people there, but two were my relatives returning from a month's vacation. Then a short time later Sigvør walked in. I have often seen her at the airport in the Faroes, either arriving or departing or picking up or delivering other passengers. This is the first time she met me in Copenhagen.

I have great admiration for the pilots who fly to the Faroe Islands. Most often the islands are covered in clouds or fog, and the tiny airport landing strip is surrounded by mountains. Yet Atlantic Air has one of the best safety records of any airline. Normally I enjoy watching out the window as my airplane is landing, but in the clouds and darkness and between mountains, I realized I was grasping the arm rest very tightly. I couldn't even see any lights, since the small terminal was on the other side of the plane.

I arrived safely and in good time in the Faroes, but my luggage didn't. With three flights leaving at about the same time, the luggage handlers in Copenhagen seemed to feel free to put Faroe Island luggage on any of the three airplanes. About a third of the people on my flight were missing luggage. I opted to stay and wait for the other two planes, which arrived about an hour later, and my luggage arrived with them.

I had arranged to have a rental car at the airport, and I had offered to take the owner of the car to his home a half hour away, since it was on my way home to Fuglafjørður, so his wife didn't have to come with a second car to the airport. He took the delay in stride, as part of life, and spent the time chatting with friends. During our wait for the luggage, the airport began filling with people coming to meet friends and relatives on the next two flights, and once again the airport was filled with sounds of noisy, talking, laughing

145

people, who all knew each other. Everyone there had had to change their plans many times during the course of the day, as changes in the weather resulted in changes to airline schedules, but everyone seemed to accept the delays cheerfully, and there was a general atmosphere of joie de vivre and good will. I have never seen anything like this in any other airport, except for Kastrup's Terminal A, gates 7, 9, and 11. Airport waiting rooms reveal something about the Faroese culture and people that I find very appealing. It is the embracing of life as it comes, valuing friends and family, and talking to anyone and everyone.

Sometimes you wait, sometimes you don't. But if you have to wait, you are fortunate if you are surrounded by Faroese friends.

Chapter 10 – Returning to the Faroe Islands

I returned home from my visit to the Faroe Islands in 1997 with 19 rolls of film, many gifts from my new-found cousins, and lots of information about the Faroe Islands and my father's family. I knew, also, that this was just the beginning, and that I wanted to return to the Faroes and bring my family. I made plans to return the following year with my husband Curtis and my brother Peter. However, my husband was unable to travel because of a recent surgery, so Peter and I went together, arriving in early August. Shortly after our arrival I was given a wonderful gift which I still treasure, a handwritten translation of all of my father's letters from his family and his sailing papers. After so many years, I was finally able to read the letters from my aunts, uncles, and grandparents and to learn a little about what my father's early life was like.

Peter met our cousins and their families and visited many of the places I had seen the previous year, and we also met new relatives and visited new places. Diana once again invited us all to dinner with her family, and as before, there was a crowd of noisy relatives in the small house. My favorite image of this visit was of her son Poul Jacob and my brother Peter playing the same accordion at the same time, Poul Jacob playing the right hand and Peter the left.

Waterfall can be seen from the old museum home in Saksun on Streymoy.

RETURNING TO THE FAROE ISLANDS

Ninna's son Henry took us on a day trip to some beautiful scenic sites on Streymoy. We followed a wide river valley across the center of the island to the small historic town of Saksun, which sits on a ridge overlooking a large bay with a very narrow opening to the western ocean between the mountains. I should say instead that the bay used to open to the ocean, until a century ago when a wild storm filled the entrance to the bay with sand, swamping and trapping a French ship that was anchored there, turning the bay into a lake. An old museum home contained a number of household items made of whale bone – kitchen utensils, hooks within the fireplace to hold cooking pots above the fire, and kitchen stools made of whale vertebrae. From the kitchen window we had a view of high waterfalls tumbling down from the mountains above. Saksun sits on a high ridge, with waters flowing both to the eastern and to the western sides of the island.

From Saksun, Henry took us back to the east side of the island and we followed the one-lane road along the coast to the northern end of the island. We could look across the narrow sound to the island of Eysturoy. In some places we had steep mountains above us on the left, and cliffs or steep slopes down to the ocean on the right. The road ended at Tjørnuvík (CHOERTnoovwick), a small town surrounded on three sides by high mountains. The fourth side was a beautiful, very cold, sandy beach, and a few miles across the water were the mountainous headlands of Eysturoy near Eiði. Along the road to Tjørnuvík, we stopped for pictures beside the Fossa waterfall and all ended up rather damp since the winds were blowing and splashing the water onto the road.

Peter was in the Faroes for two weeks, and after he left I stayed for two more weeks. I wanted the opportunity for some more leisurely sight-seeing, and after two weeks of constant visiting and being surrounded by people, I wanted a little time to be alone. I had the chance to take two wonderful trips that were different from anything else I had done.

I had read about the island of Mykines (MEEHchuhness), the westernmost of the Faroe Islands, very remote and accessible or

THE MISSING SON — A FAROE ISLAND SAGA

My brother Peter Jacobsen climbed over the guardrail to take a picture of the town of Tjørnuvík, on the northern tip of Streymoy.

RETURNING TO THE FAROE ISLANDS

weather, and I had been hoping to visit the island. Its shoreline cliffs are filled with nesting birds, some of which are found nowhere else in the Faroes. Bernhard, Poul Jacob's son-in-law, arranged to take me, and we made reservations for two nights at a guest house on the island. Bernhard had never been to Mykines, though he had made a couple of attempts when he was out fishing, but had been unable to land because of the weather.

Mykines was accessible by helicopter several times a week or by daily ferries from Sørvágar, a small town on the west side of the island of Vágar. Bernard and I drove to Tórshavn, where we left his car and caught the helicopter, but it took us only as far as the airport. Because of high winds, it wasn't safe to fly to Mykines, so we took the bus to Sørvágar, where we waited an hour or two for the ferry. The ferry was a rather small boat with about a dozen passengers, and the trip to Mykines took an hour and a half. I used a couple of rolls of film on the trip. The scenery was beautiful, a little bit of sun with dramatic-looking clouds. The Sørvágar fjord was protected and calm, but when we reached the open ocean between Vágar and Mykines the sea became rough, and the wind was strong and cold, piercing through my warmest clothes.

I stayed outside because I didn't want to miss the amazing scenery. I was fascinated by the island/rock Tindholmur, with its sheer, undercut face on the south side. The top of the ridge was jagged rock, and the north side was sharply ridged, and with the sun behind it, it was dark and foreboding. It reminded me of a sleeping dragon. Looking back toward Vágar, I could see the jagged cliffs that surrounded the island.

As we approached Mykines, all I could see of the island was miles of wind-carved cliffs above us. I could also see and hear the birds — swirling, dipping, and diving all along the face of the cliffs. Near the western end of Mykines is a small natural gorge on the south side of the island. A shelf has been cut into the rocks here to make a small dock for the boats to load and unload. When the sea is rough, there is little protection and it is unsafe for boats to attempt to dock. Stone steps lead up the side of the steep hill to the town of Mykines above the harbor in a small valley.

Puffins sit on the hillside overlooking the town of Mykines.

The island of Mykines has only one town, also called Mykines, with about two dozen buildings. There are several guest houses and some residents rent out rooms during the summer months. Only about a dozen people remain on the island during the harsh winter, and they are often cut off from the rest of the islands for months at a time. We stayed in a small guest house that had a restaurant downstairs. A steep ladder led to the upper level where four small rooms shared the space under the sharply peaked roof.

Saturday morning was bright and sunny, though the ground was damp from rain during the night, and we decided to hike out to Mykinesholmur, the western tip of the island, which was separated by a deep chasm from the rest of the island. I didn't know what I was getting

RETURNING TO THE FAROE ISLANDS

myself in for. We walked up a steep grassy slope to the crest of the hill above the village – well, I thought it was the crest of a hill, but actually it was the edge of the island, with cliffs dropping to the ocean below. We followed a trail along the ridge with cliffs on one side and a steep hillside on the other. These steep slopes were the nesting grounds for puffins that make their nests in holes in the grassy slopes. The end of August was past their main nesting season, but we still saw many thousands of the small parrot-like birds with brightly colored beaks. Wherever we had a view of the slopes, we could see the puffins lined up in rows facing the ocean, looking a little like miniature penguins. From the ocean to the top of the cliffs the air was filled with swirling currents of flying and diving birds. Flying puffins have a rather comical appearance, with short stubby rapidly whirring wings right in the middle of their bodies on each side. I saw several puffins with a row of small fish lined up evenly in their beaks, and I wondered how they caught more fish without losing the ones they already had.

Our trail then turned into steep stone stairs going down the face of the cliffs. After several switchbacks, it curved back around to the grassy slopes on the south. However, I found these slopes to be more treacherous than the cliffs. Bernhard had gone on ahead of me, and I was on my own. I wondered what a middle-aged out-of-shape woman was doing here. The slope was steep, the long grass was wet, and everything was slippery and muddy. I didn't think I was in danger of sliding down into the ocean, but I repeatedly slipped into holes hidden by the long grass. At one point I found myself thigh-deep in a muddy hole, and as I struggled (once again) to raise myself out of the hole, I realized that both of my hands were in piles of sheep dung. There was nothing else to do but to wipe my hands on the wet grass and continue on down the slope.

To get to the tip of the island we crossed a narrow bridge across the chasm, with the Atlantic Ocean roaring below us. The bridge had a gate at each end to keep the sheep out, and it was completely fenced with wire mesh fencing, including the top. I suspect this was to keep tourists from blowing away. The wildness and isolation of the landscape was mesmerizing – and this was a clear summer day. In winter this would be a desolate place indeed.

153

THE MISSING SON — A FAROE ISLAND SAGA

Eventually we made our way back up the grassy slope, up the steps on the cliff, across the ridge, and back down into the valley to the town. Going up hill on the grassy slope, at least I didn't slip and slide as often as I had going down, since the sun had started to dry out the grass.

In the afternoon I wandered up the valley the other direction from the town, toward the hilly interior of the island. There was a dirt road leading out of the village, but the only motorized vehicle I saw on the island was a small tractor. I was fascinated by the birds – countless birds on the steep cliffs on both sides of the islands. There were many kinds of birds, but the puffins were my favorite. When we went back to the guest house that evening, we had puffin for dinner – two small stringy birds for each of us.

Sunday afternoon we caught the helicopter back to the Vágar Airport. There were about 10 of us crammed into the passenger section, and I was fortunate enough to have a window seat so I could see the scenery. When the pilot realized he had a foreign tourist on board, he took the long route, going out to the tip of the island and then flying along the northern side of Mykines at about cliff-height. The view was amazing – the cliffs with carved spires and pillars, waterfalls dropping hundreds of feet to the rocky shore, rushing torrents zigzagging down deep crevasses. This wild and wonderful view is usually reserved for a few passing sailors and fishermen.

When we arrived at the airport, we found out that the helicopter was going no further, so we took the bus back to Tórshavn where we picked up Bernhard's car and drove home. We had dinner at Bernhard and Lillian's home, where the whole family was waiting for us.

Poul Jacob mentioned that I had visited most of the populated islands in the Faroes, but that I hadn't been to Suðuroy (south island), one of the larger islands both in area and population. I checked the ferry schedule and found that Wednesday was the only day the ferry left Tórshavn in the morning and then returned the same afternoon. I decided to make the trip by myself, spend a few hours walking around the town, and then return to Tórshavn. I would enjoy the longer boat ride, and I would be able to see some of the other islands from the ferry. Tuesday I stayed with my cousin Ninna, whose home was just two blocks from the Tórshavn ferry terminal. The trip to Suðuroy took

154

RETURNING TO THE FÆROE ISLANDS

nearly three hours. On the way, we passed close to several other islands, but the weather was cloudy and windy, so I stayed inside the lounge for most of the trip. Normally the ferry sailed to the town of Vágur, but on that day the ferry went to Tvøroyri instead, because of a funeral there. At first, I thought that Poul Jacob was joking when he told me that the ferry changed its destination to accommodate the people who were traveling to the funeral. I can't imagine a transportation agency in America changing its schedule to accommodate a funeral.

I was also surprised that I ended up with a private tour guide for my day in Suðuroy. After I told Poul Jacob my plans, he phoned Peter Martin from the Fuglafjørður tourist office, and Peter Martin phoned the tourist office in Tvøroyri and asked if they would be able to have a guide for a special guest from America. When I arrived my tour guide was waiting for me. Ólivur was a high school teacher of Faroese language and history, and he was a delightful guide, telling me many fascinating stories about the Faroe Islands and its history. Our first stop was his home where we had a quick lunch. When I started to tell him that father was from the Faroe Islands, he stopped me. He had read my story in the newspaper the previous year.

Suðuroy is a long narrow mountainous island, with cliffs on the western edge, and almost all of the towns were in valleys and along bays on the eastern side. Several coal mines are located in the northern mountains, and plans were underway to begin drilling for oil in the off-shore waters. In the three hours before the ferry returned to Tórshavn, Ólivur took me around the northern part of the island. From the northern hills of Suðuroy we had a good view of Stóra Dímun and Lítla Dímun, the two smallest islands in the Faroes. Lítla Dímun, which is about 1 kilometer in diameter, is uninhabited and has no harbor or access from the sea, with steep cliffs all the way around the small island. The Farmer and his family are the only residents of Stóra Dímun. Years ago, the island was used as a reform school for juvenile delinquents, and young men sent to the island had to work hard at subsistence farming and raising sheep just to survive. It was a program with no repeat offenders. Even earlier, the island had occasionally served as a prison.

The time passed quickly, and soon we had to head back to the ship. As we drove through Tvøroyri, many people who knew Ólivur

155

THE MISSING SON — A FAROE ISLAND SAGA

turned and waved. He said he would be doing a lot of explaining the next day.

On the ferry back to Tórshavn the weather was beautiful and clear, and I stood by an open window watching the passing scenery. As we approached the island of Sandoy, I asked a man next to me if he knew the name of a town we could see, explaining that I had a cousin who lived on Sandoy.

Him: *What is your cousin's name?*

Me: *Anna Katrin Jacobsen, and her husband is Torstein Holm.*

Him: *He is the dentist, right? Isn't he in Greenland now?*

Me: *No they returned about a week ago. I had dinner with Anna Katrin at her father's home in Runavík. Last year I visited them on Sandoy.*

Him: *You must be the cousin from America! I saw you on television last year.*

Then he stopped talking to me and told everyone around that I was the cousin from America who came to the Faroes and found her father's family. For a little while I felt like a celebrity – my fifteen minutes of fame. In one afternoon, two different strangers recognized me from newspaper and television from the previous year. I also was getting the impression that everyone knows everyone else in the Faroes.

When the ferry got back to Tórshavn, I walked the two blocks to Ninna's house, only to discover that she and Henry had driven down to the ferry terminal to pick me up. I walked back to the terminal, found Ninna, and rode back to her house. After dinner, Henry offered to take us to Nolsoy on his boat. The sun was setting when we left Tórshavn, and as we approached Nolsoy the town and the whole island were bathed in a warm golden glow. In the far northern latitudes dusk lasts a long time, and it takes much longer for the sun to set than it does at home. We wandered around the town, out along the rocky shore, and up the road to the fields and low hills. When we got back to the town, we stopped at a small coffeehouse to get something to drink before going back to the boat. On the dock was a fisherman with an unusual catch – young birds. When these birds leave their nests in the cliffs for the first time, they are well-fed and heavy. They can easily fly down to the ocean where they float and swim for several days while they lose weight and develop the strength to fly back up to their nests in the cliffs. The fisherman had netted several dozen of these birds, which are considered quite a delicacy. The boat ride back to Tórshavn was cold, windy and dark. Henry invited us for pancakes at his home with a view the city – a lovely ending to a wonderful day.

At breakfast the next morning Ninna's husband Jens and I were trying to talk, rather unsuccessfully. By this time I knew a few dozen Faroese words, and he knew about the same number of English words. He told me, through Ninna, that he wanted so much to talk to me that it hurt here (putting his hand on his heart) that he couldn't. I was very moved by his wish to be able to talk with me.

In 1999 my husband Curtis was finally able to go with me to the Faroe Islands, and I could introduce him to my cousins and show him first-hand the places he had seen in my photographs. Curt was just beginning to experience the effects of inoperable cancer, and he had to take it easy much of the time, so our visit was more leisurely than my previous visits, and our schedule often left time for an afternoon nap. Curt loved to hike, and he was able to take a few short hikes in the Faroe hills.

One afternoon we walked through the town and into the hills above Fuglafjørður, following a creek through grassy fields and up the mountainside. It was a warm sunny day, and the views were magnificent, with large white clouds in the deep blue sky. When we reached the steeper slopes, I kept losing my footing in the mud and grass, so I turned back to go home, while Curt continued on. As I was walking through the town, a man called to me from his doorstep. I explained that I couldn't understand him, since I only spoke English. He hurried out to talk to me, saying that his father was a very good friend of my father when they were growing up in Fuglafjørður. He invited me to come in for a glass of beer, and we talked for a few minutes before I went on home. When Curt arrived an hour or two later, he told almost the same story – about a man who was the son of my father's friend inviting him in for a beer.

Gunnleyg gave us a tour of the Gøta fish factory, which had been founded by her father. There were a dozen different areas where different types of fish were handled or where different tasks were done – cleaning, filleting, salting, freezing, packaging, and so forth. Star the art machinery helped in every step of the processing. It was fascinating to watch the automated equipment that wrapped a whole pallet of boxed and frozen fish for shipping. We also visited the offices, and Curt, as an economist, was particularly interested in the sophisticated computer systems used by the Scandinavian and northern European market for buying and selling fish while it was still on the ship, and directing the ships to the appropriate ports.

A Fuglafjørður tradition says that at midnight on the night of July 3, the waters of the Varmakelda Warm Springs, have special healing properties, so for the closing event of the Varmakelda Festival, hundreds of people walk, drive, or sail across the bay to the springs. Jørmund invited us to go in his boat, and as we were making our way through the crowds of people, I made the mistake of mentioning to someone that we were going in Jørmund's boat. Word spread quickly, and dozens of revelers crammed themselves into the small boat for a ride across the bay. All of the uninvited guests got off the boat to join the festivities on land, while we stayed on board just offshore. By the time we returned to the town, the skies were already starting to lighten with the dawn.

During the months following our trip to the Faroe Islands, my husband Curt continued to weaken from the cancer that was spreading through his body, and he died at the age of 54, five months after we returned home. During his last month, I was able to take off work and stay home with him, and our children were home with us when he died.

OVERLEAF: My father's home was near this beach in Fuglafjørður. ➤

II

Fuglafjørður, September 2006: On July 1, 2005, I retired from my job as a computer programmer, and 3½ weeks later I flew to the Faroe Islands to live for the next 13 months. Since I now had so much free time, I knew I needed a project to keep me busy, and I volunteered to help a cousin create a book of photos of his paintings. During a few months' time, I visited nearly a hundred homes and businesses, taking photos of about 140 oil paintings, all painted by my cousin during the past 40 years. The book, "Mótljós – Into the Light" by Heðin Kambsdal, published in November 2008, is in Faroese and English. Working on this book was an ongoing lesson in Faroese hospitality. I was a stranger and foreigner who spoke only a few words of their language, who invited herself into their homes; and I was always welcomed. I was offered countless cups of tea or coffee, accompanied by refreshments, and I would usually stay to visit for a few minutes or even for an hour or two.

So here I was, standing in the kitchen of a complete stranger, shoes off, coat and scarf off, wondering what I should do next. I had spoken to Mr. Petersen 20 minutes earlier, and he was expecting me, but I couldn't find anyone at home. First I had checked the garage, where lights were on and a radio playing; but no one was there. I tried the downstairs front door, but it was locked, and there was no doorbell. I walked around the house and up the hill to the back door upstairs (the family entrance to a home), went inside, and took off my shoes and coat. I went into the kitchen, and called out "Hello" several times, but there was no answer. I checked the living room and stepped down the hallway, still calling "Hello," but I hesitated to try any of the closed doors. I could hear a radio playing somewhere in the house. Not for the first time, I asked myself how I had gotten into such a predicament.

Finally, I had an inspiration. I pulled out my cell phone and called Mr. Petersen's phone number. Almost immediately the phone next to me in the kitchen rang. Finally, a door opened downstairs, and a young man answered the phone. I explained that I had come to take a photograph of a painting that the family had purchased from my cousin 25 years ago, and Mr. Petersen was expecting me. I added that, at the moment, I was standing upstairs in his kitchen. With perfect courtesy, the young man helped me photograph the painting, and by the time we finished, his father had returned home. He had gone out for a few minutes to get some fish from a neighbor who had just returned from a fishing trip. (Never turn down an offer of fresh fish.)

Another afternoon I visited Fritz to photograph a painting in his home. After I sat down, he asked whether I wanted cake or meat. I asked for the

THE NEXT GENERATION

meat, and he brought tea, coffee, bread, cheese, and dried lamb – a Faroese favorite. After we ate, I photographed the painting, and then Fritz showed me other artwork throughout the house, including many of his own oil paintings. Then we sat down at his computer and he showed me photos of an exhibition of some his paintings that were currently on display at an art gallery in a nearby town.

I experienced the kindness of relatives, friends, and strangers in many different circumstances. I would usually walk into town to do my errands; and if I was caught in the rain, often a car would stop and someone would give me a ride home. Since it rains 300 days a year, it is easy to get caught in the rain. Several times, the mail carrier delivered my groceries for me, carrying them in the mail pouch on her little motor scooter. One winter evening, my furnace stopped working, and my house started to get cold. I went to my night school language class at the high school, and mentioned my problem to another student. She phoned her husband, who phoned his cousin, who worked for one of the fuel companies, and the cousin came out to my house and got my furnace started. When I got home from class, my house was warm again, and I didn't even get charged for the service.

I lived in the Faroes long enough that I started taking the Faroese hospitality for granted. Any time I visited someone, they would offer food and drink. However, I am embarrassed to confess that I didn't get in the habit of offering hospitality to people who entered my doors. More than once, when a friend or relative would stop by unexpectedly, we would visit for a while, and as they were leaving and getting into their cars, I would suddenly remember that I had forgotten my manners. I wanted to call them back and say, "Please, would you like coffee or tea? May I get you cake or meat?"

Chapter 11 – The Next Generation

Two years later, in July 2001, my children visited the Faroe Islands with me – my son Jonathan, daughter Natasha, and her husband John. There was actually quite a crowd of us, since my brother Peter was also there with his wife Joanne. I was worried about how I would find housing and transportation for six Americans, but once again my generous cousins found a perfect solution. Esmann and Gunnleyg were going on vacation for two weeks with their entire family, and they let us use their house and two cars while they were gone. Peter and Joanne arrived first, and they had time to visit for a few days before Esmann and his family left.

Jonathan and I had been traveling in Eastern Europe with our church choir, and we met John and Natasha at the Frankfurt airport after their flight from San Francisco. We flew together to Copenhagen, and then changed planes for the two hour flight to the Faroe Islands. However, fog completely blanketed the Faroes, so the plane circled for about half an hour, and then turned around and flew to Bergen to refuel. We spent an hour and a half in an isolated terminal in the Bergen airport, and then we got back on the plane and headed toward the Faroe Islands again. I could see the mountains of the Northern Islands from the plane, but the island of Vágar, where the airport was located, was still blanketed by fog. We circled for another hour, and then we headed toward Reykjavik, where we spent the night in a hotel, courtesy of Atlantic Airways. No wonder airplane tickets to the Faroe Islands are expensive. Natasha and John had been traveling for 28 hours before they finally got to bed, and they still weren't at their final destination. Tuesday morning there were only a few high clouds, and we were able to land in the Faroe Islands with no problem. Jóan Pauli, Esmann's son, had left his car for us in the airport parking lot, and at the front desk we picked up an envelope with a key, a photo of the car, and a sketch of where to find the car in the parking lot.

This was my fourth trip to the Faroe Islands, so by this time I felt quite at home. We all appreciated having a place of our own to stay where we could relax and shed our company manners occasionally. I took my children to see some of my favorite places, and we visited with all of my first cousins, met lots of new relatives, and spent time with people I have come to love very dearly.

We all went to the Vestmanna Bird Cliffs, and though the weather was a bit foggy, the ocean was smooth, and the boat was able to take us very near the cliffs, into rocky secluded gorges with cliffs on all sides of us. On another day Gunnleyg's brother took us in his boat along the coast of Eysturoy, and we passed many familiar towns on the way and saw beautiful waterfalls. We went to the northern end of the island, where the sheer cliffs and the massive rock formation of Búgvin (575 feet high) were densely populated with noisy nesting birds. Another morning we woke up to find that the annual sheep-shearing in Gøta was going on just down the road from us, so we walked down to the sheep fold to watch. It seemed to be a family activity for people of all ages, including kindergarten children using blunt children's scissors to try to shear the sheep.

Since we had use of a nice house with a good kitchen, one evening we prepared an American dinner for Poul Jacob and his family. On my three previous trips I had stayed in their home and they had prepared many meals for me, so it was nice to have a chance to repay their hospitality. With six of us and ten from their family we had sixteen for dinner, and more people came for dessert. We could find only 15 seats for the table, so Natasha volunteered to be the hostess without a chair, and ch either stayed in the kitchen or served everyone at the table
    e meal. It was challenging to work in someone else's home,
    he food had foreign labels and the appliances had strange

symbols on them and no instructions. We were only able to get the dishwasher started when someone leaned against it and accidentally pushed some button that turned it on, so we just kept the door open until we were ready to wash the dishes. The oven had eight different controls with strange diagrams that we didn't understand, and we weren't quite sure of the temperature conversion between Fahrenheit and Celsius. We didn't really figure out how it was supposed to work until we asked Gunnleyg after she returned home. I confused corn starch and powdered sugar, which look and feel about the same, and I found myself trying to thicken my pie filling with powdered sugar. Fortunately, a little extra sugar didn't hurt the pie. Peter and Joanne stayed about a week, and they left Esmann's car at the airport for him to pick up when he returned from his holiday.

We also had a tour of the Fuglafjørður harbor and one of the fish factories, which was closed for summer holidays. We visited a factory that makes pellets for the salmon fisheries – a huge facility with monstrous tanks and many miles of pipes. The smell inside the buildings was very pungent, and my coat smelled bad for days. We also went into the freezers in caves under the mountain, where four or five huge rooms, each the size of a gymnasium, were used for storing fish and other products.

John was able to stay for a little more than one week because he needed to get back to work. In the Faroe Islands, every employee gets at least five or six weeks of vacation, and my relatives were surprised to learn that American companies sometimes give only one or two weeks of vacation a year. The day before his flight left we drove to Tórshavn to stay with Ninna, and we spent the day with her, sightseeing and visiting with her and her family. John and Natasha were anxious to try some of the Faroese food specialties before he left, but we couldn't find anything in the grocery store. In the evening, Ninna's son Henry came with wonderful Faroese foods. One of the specialties of the Faroe Islands is skerpikjøt (*SHESHPetchuht*), a leg of lamb that has been air dried all winter in a drying house with slatted walls open to the strong cold winter winds. You slice thin strips off of the leg of lamb, salt it, and eat it with bread. He also brought dried whale meat to eat with little slices of dried blubber. We also had dried fish that was air dried by hanging it outside in a shady location for several days or weeks.

We often saw fish hanging to dry on the shady side of a house, under a porch, or on a clothesline. We tried all the different foods, and my kids liked the Faroese foods. The next morning we saw John off at the airport, and fortunately his plane arrived and left on time.

Culture clash – satellite dish stands next to a clothesline used to dry laundry and to dry fish.

During the next week we took a number of sightseeing trips, and nearly every night we had a meal in the home of a different relative. Two meals were especially memorable. Jørmund was the captain of a shrimp trawler, and at his house we were served mounds of shrimp, more than we could possible eat, and we piled them high on bread. They were wonderful. After we were full of shrimp, they brought out

THE NEXT GENERATION

the main dish, which was a curried fish casserole with several kinds of fish, served over rice. At that point we realized that the shrimp were just the appetizers. We managed to make a dent in the fish casserole as well.

On another evening we were preparing to make dinner for ourselves; and I had just returned from the grocery store when the phone rang, and Heðin invited us to Tórshavn for fish soup with his niece and nephew. Of course we said yes. "Fish soup" doesn't adequately describe the wonderful food we were served, a curried dish filled with a dozen different kinds of fish and shellfish. Janhard's house was located in the oldest section of Tórshavn a block or so from the historic parliament buildings. He had bought the house about five years earlier, and was restoring it in his spare time. The house was about 400 years old, built with massive beams that were ten to twelve inches square. The small garden was on the site of a very old cemetery, and on a few occasions they had found bones when they were digging in the garden. Janhard showed us some photographs of a six month trip he had taken sailing across the Pacific Ocean on the ship skippered by the granddaughter of my cousin Hanni. Janhard sailed with them from Tahiti to many of the South Pacific Islands as far as Indonesia.

One of the places that I wanted to take my children was the island of Mykines. We took the car to the airport on Friday and left it for my cousin, who would return on Saturday or Sunday, and we left the key in the office where we had picked it up earlier. Then we took the bus from the airport to the ferry dock in Sørvágar. We planned to make the return trip with public busses and ferries – the ferry from Mykines to Vágar, the bus across the island of Vágar, the ferry from Vágar to Streymoy, the same bus halfway across the island of Streymoy, transfer to another bus that would take us the rest of the way across Streymoy, over the bridge to Eysturoy, and all the way around Eysturoy to the bus stop a block away from Esmann's house in Gøta. If everything went according to schedule, the trip shouldn't take us much longer than it would by car. I even convinced my children of this

The ferry ride to Mykines took 1½ hours, the boat was small and crowded, and the sea between the islands was very rough. We all got wet from waves crashing over the side of boat, and most of the passengers

169

were seasick. Unfortunately, we had forgotten to take our seasick pills. When we finally arrived on Mykines, the weather was foggy and drizzling. I'm sure my children were wondering why I had dragged them across several islands for this. We walked around in the rain for a while before having dinner in the dining room of the bed and breakfast. We had puffins for dinner, and again they were dry and stringy, but adding gravy and rhubarb marmalade improved the taste.

The next morning the sun was shining brightly and there was hardly a cloud in the sky. This island had millions of puffins nesting in the steep grassy slopes. Natasha and Jonathan hiked out to the western end of the island, but I abandoned them when the trail started steeply down the cliff-side and walked back to the easy trail on the other side of the town. They had lunch sitting on the rocks facing the Atlantic Ocean, with Canada somewhere ahead of them and thousands of birds flying all around them. While they were eating, Natasha noticed a puffin with fish in its mouth who landed a few feet from her and stood there for a while glaring at her. The bird flew away and returned almost immediately. When Natasha finished lunch and stood up, the puffin marched up to the spot where she had been sitting and went into a hole in the ground, bringing food to feed the baby puffins. She had been sitting over the entrance to the nest.

The Saturday afternoon ferry was very late picking us up from Mykines, and when we got back to the island of Vágar, we had missed our bus by ten minutes – the last bus on the schedule for the day. The annual Vágar festival was in progress, with boat races, vendors, and carnival rides; and it was the races that delayed the ferry. Nobody could tell us whether or not there was going to be another bus, and we were a very long way from home. I considered going to the airport and getting the car we had left for my cousin, but I didn't want to leave him in the lurch.

We made our way through the crowded streets up to the main part of town, where I left Jonathan and Natasha with our luggage and went to look for help. I stopped at a hot dog stand and found someone who spoke English. I asked him if there was a pay phone in town (no there wasn't) or if there was a way I could phone for a taxi (no there weren't any taxis, especially since there were no more flights due at the airport). I explained that we needed to get to the other side of the island to

THE NEXT GENERATION

Puffin carries a beak full of fish to feed to its young.

171

catch the Vestmanna ferry. He very kindly offered to drive us to the ferry, and when we got to the dock the ferry was just loading. We had missed the last bus going to Eysturoy, but the ferry had a telephone, so I bought a phone card and called for help. I knew only two phone numbers, so I called the one where I knew someone would speak English, Lillian and Bernhard's house. Bernhard had just returned from a three day fishing trip and was exhausted, but he agreed to meet us in Kollarfjørður (KOTlahfeeorhuh) on Streymoy, which was the closest to home we could get by bus.

Our bus was already on the ferry, so we boarded the bus before it left the ferry. Half an hour later the bus dropped us at a stop a mile or so from the town of Kollarfjørður. Since we had agreed to meet Bernhard in Kollafjørður, I thought we should walk back to the town. It turned out that this was not a very good idea. We cut across some fields and headed for the town. Just as we got back to the main road, a car stopped beside us. It was our cousin Heðin who was driving home to Fuglafjørður from Tórshavn. He offered us a ride, but I knew that Bernhard was on his way, so I said I thought we should wait for Bernhard. Heðin drove us the short distance to the town and left us at the bus stop. Just a few minutes later, we saw Bernhard drive past. We waved, shouted and jumped up and down, but he didn't see us. Heðin and Bernhard had seen each other as they passed, and they each waved, so Heðin assumed we would shortly be on our way home. We waited at the bus stop for two more hours, carefully watching every car that passed, before we saw Bernhard again, on his way back home. Once again, he didn't see us as we waved, shouted, and jumped. He had waited for us at the bus stop, had driven all the way to Vestmanna, waited for the last bus, and finally turned around and went home. By now it was after 11:00 p.m. and we were all cold and tired. Fortunately, it wasn't raining. Jonathan found a very kind person in the town who let him come in her house to use the phone, and he called Lillian again, explaining our predicament. Lillian found out exactly where we were waiting and said she would find someone to come pick us up. It was just after midnight when Heðin drove up again, three hours after he had dropped us off at the bus stop. We got home after 1:00 a.m., nine hours after we started our trip home, the trip that shouldn't take much longer by ferries and busses than it would by car.

THE NEXT GENERATION

Exhausted, we all went to bed, only to be awakened a few hours later by the ringing telephone. At 5:00 in the morning, Natasha woke up and suddenly realized she was downstairs in the kitchen, talking on the phone. Esmann's family had just arrived at the airport, and his son Jóan Pauli was calling to ask about his car. He had lost his other car key, and the one we left at the airport was locked in the office and nobody could open it. His car remained at the airport, while the whole family was able to get home with the help of the airplane pilots. They had just flown everyone from Spain to the Faroes, and then they drove them the rest of the way home in their cars.

After my previous trips to the Faroes, my children dutifully looked at my photographs, after I had organized all of the best ones. After this trip, we all sat around my dining table for hours, and we looked at all of the pictures from everyone's camera, seeing the same scene many different times.

On each visit to the Faroe Islands, I experienced the kindness and hospitality of family, friends, and strangers. However, when I think of Faroese hospitality, Hans Peter from the Hotel Eiði immediately comes to mind. On my first morning in the Faroe Islands he located my cousins for me, and on each trip to the Faroes I visited his hotel restaurant, where he graciously insisted on serving me and the others with me at no cost. On my second visit, he served us coffee and pastries. On the third visit, he served us coffee, tea, and cake. The fourth year he served asparagus soup, bread, and tea to Peter and Joanne one week and to me and my children the next. I spent two nights in his hotel in 1997, and I think I made a friend for life.

OVERLEAF: Breiðá waterfall was a quarter mile from the house where I lived in Fuglafjørður in 2005-6 ➤.

Leirvík, December 2005: *When a special event comes along, the Faroese people love to celebrate, and I have been to some wonderful parties in my time in the Faroes.*

Áshild and Petur Henry celebrated their twenty fifth wedding anniversary in December with a dinner for 300 people in a rented hall in the nearby town of Leirvík. Saturday there was a heavy snowfall, so I got a ride from a cousin to avoid having to drive in the ice and snow. I managed to embarrass myself by slipping on the ice and falling down just as we got to the door. Arriving guests were serenaded with chamber music with piano, flute, and trumpet. The meal was served family style, with large platters of food passed down the long tables. During the meal, many people made speeches toasting (or roasting) the happy couple, and after each speech, we all joined in singing a song from the printed book of songs at each place setting. The songs were in a variety of languages, Faroese, Danish, Norwegian, Swedish, and English. Dinner itself lasted from 7 p.m. until midnight.

Then tables were cleared, and we all joined in the traditional Faroese chain dance, accompanied by the a capella singing of the old Faroese Bridal Ballad. This ballad tells the biblical story of Isaac and his bride Rebecca, and it takes about 30 minutes to sing. We were led by two of the countries leading ballad singers. They would sing the verses, then the crowd joined in the refrain after each verse. Following the Bridal Ballad, we sang and danced to several other well known ballads. By 1:30 or 2 a.m. a small band started playing contemporary music, and the more modern dancing began. In the next room, there were tables of cakes, cookies, coffee, and tea, so those who didn't want to dance could talk and eat. At about 4 a.m. the tables were cleared again, and the caterers brought out breakfast – rolls, breads, cheese, marmalade, fruit, juice, and more coffee and tea, It was 5 a.m. when we headed for home. During the night, rain melted all of the snow. As we were going through the Leirvík tunnel, an empty bus passed us heading for the party. It had been hired to drive home those who were not in a condition to drive themselves.

Chapter 12 – More Love Letters

Maren continued to correspond with the sailor Hans for several more years. In 1920 letters were exchanged frequently, but there were long gaps between letters in 1921, and Hans received no letters at all from Maren in 1922. From her last two letters in 1923, it seemed that she had finally given up hope of his return.

Fuglefjord, 11 January 1920

My Dear Sweetheart,

Thanks for the letter I got from you before Christmas. You can not believe how glad we were to get a letter, since we had not heard from you for such a long time. You have to know how glad I was to hear from you, my lovely friend. You I have loved and you I will love as long as I am on this earth. My love to you will not be cool even if you are far away from me, and I will not believe that you will forget me. You must not think that I am unfaithful to you, even if there are many who are encouraging me to do it. When I have a friend that belongs in my heart, then I will live faithful to him.

My dear friend, this summer I often thought that we would not see each other again. I got pneumonia and was very ill, and I thought that my last time had come. I thought to send the last letter from me to you, but my Lord helped me. Then I wished that you were by my side, but you are so far away. The Lord saved me this time. I do not know how long a time we shall be on earth, but we have to live honorable and Christian lives, then we are ready when the Lord calls us.

My dear friend, I have been wanting to learn some trade, but I have not been so well since summer. I have been doing some sewing and I earn some money in that way. Everything is so expensive. I bought myself a sewing machine. The price was 135 Kr. Before the price was 32 Kr. Everything is expensive, but the wages are high. There is plenty of fish and the price is good.

Niels Peter Midjord went out sailing last year, and he will be coming home again. He is in Copenhagen and will come with the first ship. He says that more money can be made at home than in sailing to other countries.

Ole Hansen is also sailing. He left last year and is sailing to America, Spain, and other countries. He is engaged to Maria Hognesen, and she gets letters from him with every ship to the Faroes. He writes from every harbor he arrives in. At Christmas she got a telegram from America.

My love, you cannot believe how much I am longing for you. I wish you were here by my side tonight, but you are so far away. My dear friend, I beg you to write a little more. There is always such a long time between letters that we are afraid for you. Now I beg you something, and you must to it - that is to send me a picture of you. Please remember to do it. It may be doubtful that we will see each other again in this world, and when I go from here, the picture shall go with me.

Fuglefjord, 2 March 1920

My Dear Sweetheart,

Now the ship Tjaldur *is here today. I have to send you my regards. I wanted to get a letter with* Tjaldur, *but I got nothing. I beg you to write more, and it must not be such a long time as before - last time it was 8 months between the letters.*

Some time ago there was a dancing ball. I waited on tables, and so did Theodor Petersen. It was very nice. The next Sunday we had a ball for the people who waited on tables, and it was also very fun. If you had been with us it would have been much better, but you are so far away. You cannot believe how much I am longing for you. I wish you were here by my side, then I would be real happy.

Dear, you know that I love you with my whole heart, and to you I will give all my love. I will hope that this love to you will not be blown out. My dear, you have to write a little more, and send me a picture of you, and I will have it as a memory of you. It may be that we will never see each other again. May the Lord assure you that I will never forget you, as long as I am living.

Maybe you have heard from your parents that Jacob Martin has learned to become a captain, but he hasn't taken the exam yet. Now he is out fishing with Johan i Toftum with a ship from Vestmanna. I have no more to write this time.

Loving regards from your darling, who will be faithful until death.
From your
  Maren
Write soon.

$\sim$

Fuglefjord, 4 April 1920

My lovely friend,

Today it is a pleasure for me to write you a few words and let you know how I am. I am very well, and I wish you the same. Thank you for the letter I got from you. I was very glad for the postcard you sent to me. The ship seems to be a nice ship to sail with in the big world, and you can see so much. There it is very different from here at home, but here we are also making progress. If you come back now, you wouldn't even recognize it because there have been so many changes. I don't know much to tell you, because before Easter there is not much fun.

The ships have just gone out again for fishing. There has been bad weather, but now it is better. The Norwegian fishing ships are now beginning to come, and then we often have dances. Hansine is not dancing any more since she had a son some time ago. She is engaged to a Dane. He was here last year, and will come again soon, and I think she will go with him to Denmark. I have heard that Jacob Mohr is getting married, he is engaged to a girl from Lervig. It seems that he is very young to be married. Stejnhold is here now, and the first thing he did when he arrived was to ask for you.

My dear sweetheart, you cannot believe how much I am thinking about you, and I wish that you were here with me tonight, then I could rest in your arms. Then our hearts would beat with happiness. The love is stronger than we know, and there is our life and hope. My dear friend, you must not think that I am distrustful of you. That I would never be, and I also think the same is true of you. The person who is living a false life will never be happy.

The Lord is watching us all. My lovely friend, I send you a curl of my hair as a reminder of me. I shall go to Torshavn to get new teeth. Then I will have a photo taken of me and I will send it to you. Please send me a curl of your hair so I can have it as a reminder of you. I know that you have black hair, but I think that you may have changed very much. It is a long time that you have been away from me. I am waiting with delight to get a photo of you. I will nearly be as happy for a photo as if you came to me yourself.

Andreas Joensen also sends his regards to you. He would like to sail with the same boat that you are sailing on.

Loving regards from your loving friend,
   Maren,
Write again and send a photo. Greet your friends from me.

With the letters from Maren we found a small envelope containing a lock of light brown curly hair, wrapped in yellowed tissue paper.

Summer 1920

My Beloved Friend,
I have to call you my lovely friend, because you are the one that my heart belongs to. Today you really disappointed me, when your parents got a letter from you, and I did not get any. Maybe the reason is that for a while you have not gotten any letters from me. Or is it because you have forgotten me. If this is so, I would that I were in the grave. Why did the Lord not take me when I was sick and nearly dead. My time was not come, and I cannot believe that the Lord will give a life of sorrow, but of gladness. If I have to live my life without you, I will not be happy. It has been two months since I last got

a letter from you, and it was written 2/2. Now a long time has passed since you last wrote, and I think you are not so nice for not writing.

Maria Hognisen and Ole Hansen are engaged. He is sailing to Spain and other places. Every time the mail comes, Maria also gets a letter from him. I have always been nice to write to you, but since we have not had an address for you for a long time, then I could not write. I believe there are many letters waiting for you in Stavanger. I wrote to you as soon as I got an address, and I also sent you a photo of me. You will get a better one later. I was supposed to go to Torshavn, but I was sick, and I don't know when I will go. I don't know much news to write. The old Ole Hansen is dead. Otherwise everything is the same.

My dear friend, write to me. You know that I will never forget you as long as my heart is beating inside me. You write and beg me not to forget you, and you know that I will not fail you. I will stop writing now. I will write again as soon as I have gotten a letter from you. Andreas Joensen also sends greetings. Don't forget your own friend.

> *From Maren*
> *Write again soon.*

❧

This letter was in an envelope addressed to Hans Jacobsen, Dominion Hotel, Trail, Kanada, B.C.

❧

Fuglefjord 18 August 1920

My Beloved Friend,

Thanks for the letter that I got from you. You have to know that I was very happy when I heard from you my lovely friend. The news is not so good to hear.

The ships are all coming back from Iceland because the sea is full of mines. The times are very troubled. All the ships have come back to the Faroes without Maseppa *and* Perlod. *We have not heard a word from* Maseppa. *None of the ships that have arrived have seen* Maseppa, *and therefore we are concerned about them. Johannes, your sister's husband, is with* Maseppa *and other men from Eide also are. Your sister is in low spirits. I feel for her. A ship from Sudero has sailed on a mine, and the other ships have found the wreckage.* Nordlyset *arrived with a mine on deck, which was very dangerous. It was very sad about Andreas Andreasen and Hilda. Hilda has been well all summer, and she worked in the fishery and other things. Some time ago she went mad, and it seems that she will not be well again. Why, is not so easy to say, but the doctor says that maybe she has worried too much or she has been reading and thinking too much. She is out and around now, but she can't understand that Andreas has come home from Iceland. It is very sad for him to meet her in this condition again. She was well when he sailed to Iceland, and she was to be his bride when he came home again. Their house is finished being built. We all would wish other things for them. He said that it would have been better if he had followed her to the grave than for this. He visits her all the time, but she does not know who he is. My dear friend, so it goes for some people; many get troubles in their youth. Love is stronger than we know. My dear friend you know that I love you and never will forget you, and I also hope that you never will forget me. I know that you also have loved me; never let it be turned off.*

I was by a photographer's when I was in Torshavn on holiday, and I had a picture taken of me and my sister Ella, but I have not gotten them back yet. I hoped that there would be a picture of you in the last letter. Your mother asked if I had a picture of you, and I said no. She said that she could not understand why you did not send a picture. Remember to send me a picture. You must not think that I will have it on exhibit.

My dear friend, I am well and I wish you the same. I always have enough to do. I have not worked in fish for two years. I am only sewing. You write that you have not gotten a letter from me. I cannot understand why. I wrote immediately after I got a letter from you. Remember, don't let so much time pass between letters. Loving wishes from your friend who will never forget you.

Maren

Remember to write. Forget me not. Be well. I will soon write again with more news.

MORE LOVE LETTERS

October, 1920

My Beloved friend,

Today I will write to you and let you know that I am well and I wish you the same. I wrote to you in the last letter that they were afraid for Maseppa, *but they have come home now. My dear friend, thanks for the letter. I was very glad when I got it. It is my greatest happiness to hear from you, my love. I am often thinking about you, and I wish that you were here, then we would be happy, but you are so far away. But even if you are far away, you are always near my heart. It is nearly 4 years since you left.*

My dear friend, I do not have so much news. Things are the same with Hilda. She is in the hospital in Klaksvík. My dear friend, I am now with my sister Andrea. She had a son yesterday. I have so much to do. I have not gotten the pictures yet. If I had I would send one to you. You must write again as soon as you can.

Friendly and loving regards from your friend,

Maren

Regards from Andrea and Olevinns. Andreas is sending a postcard to you.

༽

Fuglefjord, 12 November 1920

My dear friend,

I will now write a few words and let you know how I am. Next Sunday there will be a wedding here, Thomas Jensen and Sofie Johannesen and Kristian Thomsen and Nicoline Olsen. The brides shall wear white silk dresses that I am sewing. I have much to do before Sunday.

Last night I went to a meeting where we wished to start a seamen's home here in Fuglefjord. I think that is a good idea. Often there are many seamen here. It is not always so easy for the seamen, and it would be good for them to have a home to come to when they are here. We are also trying to get a doctor here, and maybe it will not be too long before we have one.

Much has changed here since you left. Last summer nine houses were built. Gjogvara and Gard streets have grown together. On the other side of the firth toward Bakka many houses have been built also.

THE MISSING SON — A FAROE ISLAND SAGA

The fishery has been bad this year. On Suderoy it was very sad; two ships were lost, and one ship from Klaksvík, Karen, Helene, *and* Kristine. *The men who were with* Kristine *are mentioned on the list I am sending you. Maybe you know some of them.*

My dear friend, thanks for the letter I got from you. You cannot believe how glad I was. The best that can happen to me is to get a letter from you, my love. You know that I love you and that the love will never burn up, even if you are so far away from me. You are always in my thoughts. I wish that you were here by my side, then I would be happy, but you are so far away, and I wish that some time we will meet each other again. The Lord has to show us the way. I will go on praying for you, and I hope the Lord may hear me, and that nothing bad will happen to you.

My dear friend, you must excuse me, since I have not much time to write now. I will write again soon. Friendly and lovely regards from your own friend,

    Maren

Be well and write again soon. Some time ago Theodor Petersen went to Bilbao in Spain, where he is living now.

≈

My father's papers included the newspaper clipping listing the sailors who were lost at sea with the Kristine.

≈

Fuglefjord, 15 December 1920

My Dearest Sweetheart,

I will now write you some words and let you know how I am. I am very well and wish you the same. I do not have much news. One thing I have to tell you about is the wedding. It was very nice. We had decorated the church with flowers, and then we followed two by two (man and woman) into the church, six couples for each. The women were in white dresses. I was in the wedding ball for Thomas and Sofie and I followed with Simon Olivar. He is an elegant boy. He is living in Torshavn and is learning to become a cabinet maker, and Poul his brother is learning to skipper. We had a lot of fun this evening. Hilda and Andreas also would have been married if she had not been ill. But now it is going better with Hilda, and we hope that she will be well again.

This year in the Faroes we have lost a ship again. It is number 4 for this year: two from Suderoy, one from Klaksvík, and one from Torshavn. Many are in sorrow and many young beautiful eyes have closed. I enclose a list of the men from the last ship. Maybe you know some of them.

My lovely friend, you know that I love you, and my love for you will never blow out, even if you are so long away from me, and you will live in my thoughts. There will never go a day that I will not think about you. It makes me so happy to know that you are well. Often there has gone a long time between letters, and then I thought that you were not well. I hope that the Lord may hold his hand over you so nothing bad will touch you where you live in the big world. The person the Lord holds his hand over will be well. I wish that the Lord will lead you happily back to me again.

My beloved friend, thanks for the letter I got from you. You have to know that it is lucky for me to hear that you are well. The loveliest that can happen to me is to get a letter from you, my sweetheart. You are far away from me, but in thoughts you are by my side.

Andreas Joensen sends wishes and he asks if you have gotten a postcard from him. It came inside a letter from me in October.

My dear friend, excuse me for writing the letter in a hurry. I will stop writing for now. Best wishes from your lovely friend,

    Maren

And I will wish you a Merry Christmas. Be well.

                          ｃ◇

We have a newpaper clipping about the sinking of the ship *Puritan* from Tórshavn. We also have the post card from Andreas, with a photograph of the bird cliffs.

                          ｃ◇

Fuglefjord, 23 January 1921

My lovely friend,

I will now write you a few words and let you know how I am. I am well and wish you the same. Today is Sunday, and I have been to the celebration of holy communion. I would have wished that you were kneeling by my side at the Lord's table to clean your heart. While I was at the Lord's table I prayed for you. I prayed not only for my sin, but also for yours. I wish that the Lord may hear me and that nothing bad will happen to you! My dear friend, you know that I love you with all my heart, and I will never forget you, as long as my heart is beating in my breast. My love to you is warm all the time. I wish you were here so I could speak to you, but you are so far away.

Andreas Joensen is sending you greetings. He asks if you have not gotten a postcard he sent to you in October inside a letter from me. He has been wanting you to answer. He was at the post office and got my letter. He was sure that inside there would also be a card for him, but there was not. Do you get the letters I am sending to you. You seldom mention that you have gotten them.

Do you have a photo of yourself. Remember to send me a photo. I am still waiting. My pictures were sent to Copenhagen for development.

I must stop now. With kind and lovely regards, from your friend,
*   Maren*
Write again soon. Now it is so lovely that we get a letter from you so often.

∞

Fuglefjord, 21 July 1921

My dear friend,

I will now write some words and thank you for the letter I got from you. I thought that you no longer cared to write to me, and that you have quite forgotten me, because it has been such a long time since I last heard from you. It has been more than half a year since you last wrote to me, so it seems that you have forgotten both me and your home. So often I have thought that you have forgotten me, but I hope that it is not so. Now I will ask you to say for sure if you are going to forget me. Even if it is so, it will be difficult for me to forget you.

My dear beloved friend, you must not be offended that I am asking. It is because I felt myself a little unsure. I would be so happy if I had a photo of you, but it seems that you will not send me one. You could show me that honor, since we have been friends for such a long time. I would not think that you would go so far away. It may not be your opinion, but the person who is going out in the big world may come to a place where he does not wish to come. My beloved friend, my thoughts always float around you. I never will forget you. It is impossible to drag you out of my heart. I am always thinking about you, now when you are so far away. I will pray to the Lord, that he shall hold his hand over you, so nothing bad shall happen to you.

My love, I will stop writing now, and I will write again soon.

From your lovely friend,

Maren

Fuglefjord

Remember to send me a photo.

༄

Fuglefjord 21 August 1921

My dear friend,

I will now write a few words and let you know that I am well, and I wish you the same. My dear friend, you have to know that for me it is very sad never to see you. I am therefore very confused. I have had a great love toward you, and all the time I have wished that it never will be blown out. Now I do not feel so sure of you. Maybe there is one who is nearer your heart than I.

My dear friend, that is one thing that I have to say to you, that is that you have to hold on to God. Only he can save our souls. We know all in this world is only nothing. We are here only for a while, therefore we have to live a Christian life, and when we are taken from here, then we will have eternal delight. My dear friend, I know that you were a Christian when you left, but it can be otherwise when you are going out in the great world. You have always sailed. Maybe you have never been in any church since you left. Then it is easy to forget everything.

My dear friend, we are waiting for a photo of you. I think it is a little strange that you have not sent a photo. Soon it will be five years since you left. Is it because of me that you will not send a photo? I think it seems so. Your mother asked me when you will come back again, and if I have not gotten a photo of you. It was very difficult to answer her that I did not know when you are coming, and no, I have not gotten a photo from you. She is very sad

THE MISSING SON — A FAROE ISLAND SAGA

Maren, my father's fiancée, wrote to him for seven years.

MORE LOVE LETTERS

now when you are so far away. She said that she thought that you never will come home again.

I will stop now. Kind regards from your
    Maren
    Do not forget Jesus. You know he will never forget you. Write again as soon as possible.

∽

Fuglefjord, 18 January 1923
My dear lovely Hans.

Thanks for the letter I got from you today. It is not nice of me that I have not written often to you recently. I do not know why. I have sat down and written a little, then there are always other things to do first, and then I have been so late to post it that the ship has gone. This time I know that I will finish the letter. It is not because you are forgotten in my heart. You will always live there. I am always thinking about how nice you were toward me when we were together.

I will be honest and I have to say that often bad thoughts are in my mind. The bad thoughts are saying to me that it is stupid of me to think about you any longer, for it seems that you will never come home again, but I cannot believe it.

My dear friend, it is true that you always will live in my heart. Every time I am in church and am at the communion table, first I am praying for you that the Lord may hold his hand over my friend who is so far away in the big world. My dear, are you following Jesus, or the world? We know the happiness in the world is only for a short time, happiness in heaven is life forever and ever. I know you were a good person when you left, but if you are wandering with bad people, you have to be strong. The world is bad, the war is dangerous, and it doesn't look good.

My dear friend, much has changed here since you left. Last Sunday Hans Hansen and Malena, the farmer's daughter, were married, and there was a wedding party. Jacob Frans, son of Albert, has also married a girl from Lervig. Sigmund and Rakul were married last autumn. Andreas Joensen is not married yet. He is engaged to Johanne. He sends his greetings. Last autumn when the ship, Nordlyset, *sailed to Grimsby, the ship sailed on land*

THE MISSING SON — A FAROE ISLAND SAGA

and sank. Everybody drowned. Three men were from Fuglefjord - Fredag Petersen, Martin (Thomas Johan's son), and Ole Jacob from Geitagard; three from Lervig and one from Gøta. Last Sunday evening the priest prayed for them in the church. It was a lovely speech. He talked about our need to be ready to go when the Lord calls for us.

I have to stop now. Friendly and loving regards from your dear friend,
Maren

Remember to send a photo of you. I would send one from me, but it seems that I should not force you with more from me when I have nothing from you. You must have taken a photo of yourself. I cannot believe that you have not.

༝

Fuglefjord, 8 August 1923

My dear beloved friend,

Thank you for the letter I have received from you. I am well and wish you the same. My dear friend, you know that I have loved you with all my heart, and my longing for you has been so great that it is impossible to say. I have comforted myself with the thought that one day I will be happy beside you. You are always in my heart, and I cannot give it to another when you are always there. Many people are saying to me "Don't be faithful to Hans any longer, it is only a delusion." I answer that I do not believe that my being faithful to you will harm you.

My dear beloved Hans, I will now ask you seriously, and I want you to answer me seriously. Do you seriously mean that you will come home to me again, or not. I have often wondered, but I cannot get any result without you answering me honestly. I do not believe that you have forgotten me, just as I have not forgotten you. I believe that our love is more like kindness than anything else, but my dear, I will be honest and tell you all.

There is a man who is trying to win my heart, but he has not gotten any answer yet. The last time he asked me, I promised to give him an answer when he comes back this autumn. It seems that he really means it, because today I got a telegram from Iceland from him. I do not want him to meet me when he comes home, therefore I will go to Torshavn. I could be engaged to him if you had not gotten my heart. He is a nice boy. He has learned to be a skipper. I could tell you who it is, but he is not from this village, and you do not know him.

My dear Hans, it was you who got my first love, and this love has been beautiful until now. Now it seems that my fortune is to be lost. I demand that you now give me an honest answer.

Write again as soon as you have gotten this letter, but you have to send it to Fuglefjord. I shall tell Simon Pauli (the postman) to send it to me. He is always so kind to hide the letters when I am not at home.

Now at last, kind and lovely regards from your loving friend,
Maren

∾

This was the last letter from Maren. She had tried everything. She told Hans she loved him. She sent greetings from his friends. She talked about engagements and weddings. She sent him news clippings about lost ships and lost sailors. She let him know about his mother's illness, her own illness, and sick neighbors. She mentioned her old boyfriend. She tried, guilt, nagging, jealousy, and love, but in the end, she failed to win back her sweetheart, Hans.

OVERLEAF: Hans Jacobsen purchased a brand new 1929 Chevrolet in San Francisco. ➤

*r, **March, 2006:** Let me tell you about a typical day for this
ving in the Faroe Islands. I am retired now, so I wake up without
lock, when I have had enough sleep. How nice! Usually I have
oatmeal, fruit, and coffee for breakfast. The Faroese usually have bread, cheese,
and marmalade, but I really don't like cheese for breakfast. During breakfast
I read the San Francisco Chronicle and the West County Times on the internet,
and I check the Faroe weather forecast. From the window by my dining table,
I can see that during the night a new ship has arrived at the harbor across the
bay and is unloading the catch of fish. I get my binoculars to check the name
of the ship to find out if one of my cousins has returned home. I also spend a
few minutes watching the flock of water birds and eider ducks catching fish in
the bay just over my back yard fence. A few times I have seen a seal playing
there. After breakfast, I carry a load of laundry down the street to Jørmund
and Bjørghild's house to use their washing machine. Later I will hang the
clothes to dry on a rack in the spare bedroom downstairs.

I walk to town (almost a mile) to do a few errands. I stop at the post office
to pay my telephone bill. My neighbor Hallbjørg is working today, and she
talks to me very slowly and simply in Faroese. I can actually understand her,
but I answer in English. When I try to talk in Faroese, no one understands
me. My next stop is the little clothing store where I bought some yarn several
weeks ago. It took all three employees in the store to help me figure out what to
buy for my American knitting pattern. I want to show them my new sweater.
They are delighted to see what I have made, and I am glad that I have a
new wool sweater. Wool sweaters and wool socks are an important part of my
wardrobe here in the Faroes. I stop at the ATM at the bank across the street
to get some kroner from my Bank of America account in Berkeley.

As I pass Poul Jacob's house, I see him at the window, so I stop to visit for
a few minutes. He is my cousin, and I have stayed in his home several times
on visits to the Faroe Islands. Jutta offers me tea and cakes. My next stop
is the grocery store. Gurið, Poul Jacob's daughter, is working today, so we
talk for a while. Her 8 year old daughter has just finished school for the day,
and she smiles and waves. Children start to learn English at about age 10 or
11, and she doesn't know much English yet. The grocery store can be quite a
language challenge, and sometimes I have to ask for help. Fortunately, several
of the clerks speak English. A few items are labeled in Faroese, but most are
in Danish. I am working hard to learn Faroese, but I don't plan to learn
Danish. Food is imported from Denmark, and it arrives in the islands on the

Monday morning ferry every week. I often buy a Faroese newspaper to practice my language skills. Since I have a mile to walk home, I try to remember not to buy too much at one time.

There is a bench overlooking the beach at the end of the bay about half way home, and I sit there for a few minutes to rest. As usual I bought too many groceries, and my arms are tired. The woman who delivers the mail comes by on her little blue motor scooter, and we talk for a few minutes. She offers to deliver my groceries, along with the mail, and I put my grocery bags in the mail pouch hanging on the front of the scooter. She says that she will be to my house in about 20 minutes.

I eat my main meal in the middle of the afternoon, and while I am eating, I read another chapter in my Faroese translation of the first Harry Potter book, with my Faroese/English Dictionary in one hand. I fetch my laundry from Bjørghild's washing machine. No one is home, but they don't lock their door. Then I spend some time checking my email, uploading new photos on my computer, and selecting the ones I want to put on my website.

Tuesday night is choir rehearsal for the Gøta-Leirvík choir in the next town. The director is my cousin, and he usually gives me a ride. I can see his house across the bay, and when his car pulls out of its parking place, I know it is time to get my coat and my music and walk up my narrow, one-lane street to the main street above me. We sing quite a few traditional Faroese songs, and this is a great way for me to learn how to pronounce this difficult language. We also have some music in English, but even the music in German or Latin is a relief to sing after trying to sing in Faroese. There are about 20 people in the choir. The two who live in Leirvík have to leave 10 minutes before the rehearsal is over because the tunnel to Leirvík closes for repair work at 10:00 p.m. If they are late, they will have a long drive on a narrow one-lane road around the mountain to get home.

After choir, I phone a friend in California. There is an eight hour time difference, so I often phone late at night. Using Skype on my computer, I can talk for an hour for just a little more than one dollar – quite a bargain. Then I finally get to bed at 1 a.m.

Chapter 13 – Epilogue

All of my life I was curious about the Faroe Islands and I wondered what life was like there. After my first amazing visit when I found my father's family, I was anxious to return and bring my family, and the pull of the Faroes has grown stronger with every trip. In the summer of 2005 I retired from my job as a programmer at the University of California Medical Center in San Francisco, and I decided to make a longer visit to the Faroes. I lived in Fuglafjørður for nearly 14 months, in the little house on the edge of the bay that had belonged to my cousins Petra and Jacob Hansen. Since that time, I have spent several months of each year in the Faroe Islands.

Hans Jacobsen met Susan Starns in 1923 in a small waterfront mission in San Francisco, where she was working as a Salvation Army officer. The prayers of my father's family were answered in this mission, as Hans made a commitment to live his life as a Christian. He continued attending services at the mission for several years, and he also fell in love with Susan. However, in 1927 she married Harold Miller, another officer in the Salvation Army, and they moved to Arizona.

Susan wrote to her parents after she moved to Arizona, and her letter included a list of some of the wedding gifts she had received. I wonder if the sailor who gave her such lovely gifts might be my father.

THE MISSING SON — A FAROE ISLAND SAGA

〜

May 23, 1927

Dearest Folks,

. . .

We have received a few more gifts since we left San Francisco. The man that gave me the Japanese kimono sent me a whole linen outfit, some of the most beautiful things I ever saw, a wonderful bedspread, linen with open-work and embroidery all over it. It is of such pure linen you can see through it. Also a linen luncheon set with 6 napkins, all embroidered; a hand towel, linen and embroidery and lace; six linen handkerchiefs, all lace and embroidery. Four real linen gowns with the most wonderful work on them, and a silk princess slip and combination suit, embroidered around the top and bottom with open work of floral spray. There was also a hat in the package, folded up, made of woven white straw with a fringe on the brim. I don't know what kind of straw it is, but it looks like linen, so I thought it may be flax. The things are certainly wonderful. He is on the sea almost all year round. He came in about Christmas time last year, and has been away until a week or so ago. He came in just after we left, so I didn't see him.

. . .

> *Much love,*
> *Susan*

〜

After my father's death, when my mother was selling the family home, she gave me the linen luncheon tablecloth that she had received as a gift for her first marriage. I wonder if it was a gift from my father.

After Susan moved away, Hans began attending services at Glad Tidings Temple in San Francisco, which had a large Bible College. He was an active member the church's orchestra, playing either the saxophone or the mandolin for church services and concerts. By co-incidence, my husband's father also played the saxophone in the same orchestra during the mid 1930's. Hans began working as an iron and steel worker beginning in 1933, work which he continued until his retirement. He worked on two projects that have become San Francisco landmarks – the Waldo tunnel just north of the Golden Gate Bridge in Marin County, and the Lincoln Tunnel, which is part of the San Francisco approach to the bridge. He told us that he drove across the Golden Gate Bridge on the day that it opened in 1937.

In 1938, Susan was left a widow with 6 young children, and she decided to move back to Oregon to be with her mother. On the way to Oregon, she stopped in San Francisco to visit her sister, and she also paid a call on Hans. After this visit, they corresponded by mail, and during the summer of 1941, Hans visited her in Gold Hill, Oregon, and asked her to marry him. After he got home, he wrote the following letter.

ᕤᕤ

San Francisco, July 20, 1941

Dear,

Left Gold Hill under the cover of darkness and traveled without sunshine some 100 miles through fog, sometimes lights and wipers going. It was not San Francisco fog, it was Oregon fog. Didn't get any sunshine until about 30 miles south of Crescent City, but from there on, it was all sunshine.

The trip was good. Got to San Francisco at 4:10, a little tired and sleepy, but it was nothing a good night's rest would not fix.

I have reservations for you in Brisbane Alito Court, only about 1½ miles from my place. Please come at once.

Sincerely yours,

H. Jacobsen

P.S. Be sure and count all the children twice, so not one will be missing.

ᕤᕤ

Hans and Susan were married in September 1941, eighteen years after they first met. Hans acquired a ready-made family of six children: Roberta 13 years, Miriam 11 years, Stanley 9 years, Susan 7 years, Erma 6 years, and Harold 4 years. Hans and Susan had two more children – Peter in November 1942 and Jennifer in April 1946.

Hans lived the rest of his life near the San Francisco Bay, within sight of the Pacific Ocean.

In February 1927, three and a half years after her last letter to Hans, Maren married Poul Petersen from Oyndarfjørður, the man she wrote about in her letter. They lived in Fuglafjørður where they raised their family. Poul Jacob was friends with Maren's son Peter Andrew, and I finally met him during my visit to the Faroes in 2006. Maren died in December 1976, just a few years before my father. She didn't ever completely forget him. During her final illness, as her mind wandered farther and farther back in time, she would sometimes speak about Hans, the sailor she had loved when she was a young woman

My relatives in the Faroe Islands have often asked me if I know why my father never returned to his homeland. Since he never talked about his past, I can't say for sure what his reasons were, but after reading his letters and hearing his stories, I can make some guesses. I think there were several different factors that influenced his decision to stay in America. First and last there were the economic reasons. Life was very difficult in the Faroes during World War One and the years following, and the letters from his family mention many hardships they endured. Second, I suspect that he was no longer in love with Maren and had decided that he didn't want to marry her. Her devotion to him made it difficult for him to tell her this, so he took the coward's way out, and didn't return. Third, he had met another woman in San Francisco whom he did love. By the time she married another man in 1927, he was already settled into a new life in America. After his marriage in 1941, he was responsible for providing for a family of eight that soon grew to ten, and it would have been impossible for him to return because of the great expense. Going from San Francisco to the Faroes was a very, very long and expensive sea voyage.

During my first visit to the Faroe Islands, there were times when everything happening seemed unreal. After a lifetime of wondering about the Faroe Islands, I had finally found the islands, and they were more beautiful than I could ever have imagined. More than that, I had found my father's family, and they had welcomed me into their lives with kindness, generosity, and love.

EPILOGUE

Føroyar,
I am drawn, pulled, yes compelled to return to you.
This primal yearning knows neither logic nor reason.

Your fierce winds both batter and revive me.
Torrential rains refresh, yet chill me to the core.
Your wild beauty, veiled by fog and mist,
returns again to catch me unawares.

Green hills that welcomed and embraced,
with season's change are barren, wind-swept slopes.
Steep cliffs, deep fjords, that captivate and awe,
ravaged by winter's storm expose their deep-ridged bones.

Your seas bring life and death, abundance and destruction.
Yet here within their boundaries is life full and rich.
Speech, not understood, gives comfort and contentment,
as mother's heartbeat does the newborn child.

I, a stranger here, was welcomed and embraced;
strong ties now knit my heart to those I love.
While far away, I'm longing to return.

Appendix 1

Sailing Records for Hans Jacobsen

Dates/Ship	Locations
January 1917 – 27 June 1917 *Guri*, from Stavanger, Norway	Norway
1918 *Guri*, from Stavanger, Norway	Norway
11 June 1918 to 30 September 1918 *Southwood*, from Middlesbro, England	Engaged in Haugesund Norway. Discharged in Aalesund Denmark. Stops in London, Hull, and Blyth England and Hvaag Norway.
April 1919 to March 1921	
29 April 1919 *M/S Kurt*, from Skien, Norway	Discharged in Bergen
May 1919 to March 1921 *Otta*, from Bergen, Norway	Engaged in Bergen, Norway. Discharged in Emden, Germany. Voyage to Vancouver, Canada.
9 April 1921 to 21 May 1921 *City of Vancouver*, from Vancouver, B.C., Canada	Engaged in Emden, Germany. Discharged in Vancouver.
January 1922 to 27 June 1922 *S/S Remus*, from Kristiania, Norway, Latin America Line	Discharged in Los Angeles, California Went ashore in San Pedro. Letter from Callao Peru near Lima.

APPENDIX I

Notes
Certificate of Discharge: Hans Jakobsen has sailed as a sailor with the schooner "Guri" for six months and has performed his work satisfactorily.
Handwritten Discharge notice says Hans Jacobsen served for 13 months as sailor and second officer.
*Certificate of Discharge. Served in capacity of sailor. *Account of Wages for August and September, withdrawing cash at Hull and Hvaag. *Letter to parents from Honningsvaag Norway on 19 September 1918, en route to Trondheim.
Member of Norwegian Seamen's Union, as a deckman.
Hans Jakobsen has, as second mate and sailor, been a reliable man during the time he has been on board "Kurt".
*Hans Jacobsen served as Mate on board the steamer "Otta" of Bergen from May 1919 to March 1921. He has served for the last seven months as Boatswain. He has always shown his fitness, carefulness, and is a trustworthy man, and takes great interest in the welfare of the ship, and carries out all orders willingly. He was paid off on account of the ship being laid up for repairs. *This was Hans' first trip to America. *Letter from Thomine in 1919 to S/S Otta forwarded from Bergen to Nice, France.
*Certificate of Discharge for Seamen, Marine and Fisheries Department of Canada. Served in capacity of Fireman. Conduct and character, very good. *An Account of Wages for 93.60 pounds.
*US Dept of Labor Immigration Service in San Pedro California: This certifies that Hans Jacobsen is qualified to land, having been discharged. *Certificate: Sailor Hans Jacobsen has sailed with S/S Remus from Kristiana for about 6 months. It is a pleasure for me to recommend him as a nice, sober, careful man. He has always done very satisfactory work. It is his wish to be discharged. *Letter to parents 9 April 1922 from *Remus* from Callao, Peru.

Dates/Ship	Locations
29 June 1922 to 8 November 1922 *Bearport*, from Portland, USA	Discharged in San Francisco.
24 November 1922	San Francisco
January 1923 to March 1925	
5 December 1922 to 9 April 1923 *Bearport*, from Portland, USA	Discharged in San Francisco. Stops in Honolulu, American Samoa, Kobe, Shanghai, Hong Kong, Swatow, Yokohama, Zamboanga, New Castle, Djakarta, Surabaji, Padang, Singapore.
2 May 1923	San Francisco
31 July 1923 to 18 September 1923 S. S. *Ventura*, from San Francisco, USA	Voyage to Sydney. Discharged in San Francisco.
17 October 1923 to 30 November 1923 *Sequoia*, from San Francisco, USA	Engaged and discharged in San Francisco.
10 June 1924 to 29 July 1924 S. S. *Ventura*, from San Francisco, USA	Voyage to Sydney. Discharged in San Francisco.
July 1924 to March 1925 *Calebra*, from San Francisco, USA	

Notes
*Certificate of Discharge. Hans Jacobsen served as an able-bodied seaman. Character, Ability, and Seamanship – very good. *Several photos from *Bearport*.
United States Certificate of Service to Able Seaman for service on the high seas and inland waters.
Member of International Seamen's Union of America, Deck Department.
*Certificate of Discharge. Hans Jacobsen served as an able-bodied seaman. Character, Ability, and Seamanship – very good. *Hans said that this ship carried cargo of wild animals from Singapore to Los Angeles.
United States Certificate of Efficiency to Lifeboat Man.
*Certificate of Discharge. Hans Jacobsen served as an able-bodied seaman. Character, Ability, and Seamanship – very good. *Letter to parents 5 July 1923 included photo of *Ventura*, noting that he served as quartermaster, and they were on the way to Sydney.
*Department of Commerce, Lighthouse Service. Certificate of Discharge, position of Seaman. *Ship supplied provisions to light houses along the California coastline.
Certificate of Discharge. Hans Jacobsen served as quartermaster. Character, Ability, and Seamanship – very good.
There is a notation in his immigration papers about Hans serving on the *Calebra*. This is probably the pilot ship Hans served on in the San Francisco Bay.

Appendix II

Jacobsen Family Tree
Descendants of Joen Magnus and
Nicoline Susanne Jacobsen

Joen Magnus Jacobsen, male, born: 10 Feb 1853, died: 24 Sep 1927, married to Nicoline Susanne Klein, female, born: 26 Feb 1854, died: 03 Apr 1934

1) Jacob Sigvald Jacobsen, male, born: 16 Oct 1880, died: 26 Feb 1900

2) Malena Jacobsen, aka: Lena, female, born: 22 Jul 1882, died: 04 Mar 1956, married to Johannes Hansen, male, born: 24 Dec 1884, died: 24 Jan 1963
   a) Jacob Sigvald Hansen, male, born: 09 Aug 1909, died: 11 Apr 1983, married to Petra Franciska Hansen, female, born: 18 Oct 1912, died: 18 Apr 2002
   b) Jógvan Frederik (Hansen) Kambsdal, male. born: 31 Jul 1911, died: 25 Dec 1965, married to Hansina Johannesen, female, born: 09 Aug 1914, died: 25 May 2007
      i) Maria Kambsdal, female, born: 22 Aug 1941, married to Petur J. Eliasen, male, born: 26 Feb 1941
      ii) Lena Kambsdal, female, born: 13 Jan 1945, died: 12 Jul 2002
      iii) Heðin Kambsdal, male, born: 14 Mar 1951

THE MISSING SON — A FAROE ISLAND SAGA

    c) Magdalena Hansen, aka: Magda, female, born: 19 May 1913, died: 26 Feb 1980, married to Jacob Lambaa, male, born: 01 Oct 1911, died: 19 Sep 1987
- i) Petrina Lambaa, aka: Dinna, female, born: 30 Aug 1937, married to Martin Eliasen, male, born: 27 Oct 1936, died: 29 Aug 2007
- ii) Oluffa Lambaa, female, born: 16 Aug 1939, married to Jógvan Ólasen, male, born: 03 Jul 1941, died: 2002
- iii) Marjun Lambaa, female, born: 17 Oct 1945, married to Johan Heri Joensen, male, born: 14 Jun 1945
- iv) Johannus Lambaa, male, born: 24 Apr 1953, married to Birita Joensen, female, born: 03 Feb 1956
- v) Jørmund Lambaa, male, born: 18 Aug 1954, married to Bjørghild Arnholdtsdóttir, female, born: 07 Dec 1958

    d) Petrina Hansen, female, born: 1920, died: 1937

    e) Poul Jacob Hansen, male, born: 29 Jul 1922, died: 21 Aug 2007, married to Jutta Larsen, female, born: 26 Feb 1923, died: 23 Jun 2007
- i) Johannes Hansen, male, born: 02 Sep 1949
- ii) Lillian Hansen, female, born: 18 Aug 1955, married to Bernhard Samuelsen, male, born: 11 Sep 1953
- iii) Gurið Hansen, female, born: 07 Jun 1967, married to Dan Samuelsen, male, born: 30 Jul 1965

3) Poul Jacob Jacobsen, male, born: 06 Aug 1884, died: 07 Jun 1916

4) Johannes Pauli Jacobsen, aka: Hannes, male, born: 10 May 1887, died: 18 Sep 1971, married to Anna Margretha Clementsen, female, born: 1889, died: Nov 1924

    a) Nikolina Jacobsen, aka: Lina, female, born: 18 Oct 1913, died: 18 Mar 1996, married to Ole Jacob Carl Christiansen, male, born: 15 Apr 1908, died: 05 May 1945
- i) Margretha Christiansen, female, born: 15 Sep 1936, married to Petur Mohr, male, born: 03 Oct 1935
- ii) Kristian Oluf Christiansen, male, born: 13 Nov 1938, married to Hanna Hentze, female, born: 05 Oct 1944

APPENDIX II

iii) Jonna Christiansen, female, born: 25 Aug 1940, died: 17 Nov 2007, married to Hans Jakob Thomsen, male, born: 03 Apr 1930, died: 09 Jun 2007, Divorce

iv) Ole Jacob Carl Christiansen, male, born: 29 Jul 1945, married to Tóra Hansen, female, born: 26 Feb 1948 *2nd Husband of Nikolina Jacobsen, Jógvan Kristiansen, male, born: 17 Nov 1919, died: 22 Oct 1995

v) Petur Henry Kristiansen, male, born: 23 Jul 1953, married to Áshild Hansen, female, born: 28 Jul 1962

b) Poul Jacob Jacobsen, male, born: 05 Jul 1916, died: 08 Sep 1936

c) Diana Jacobsen, female, born: 03 Oct 1918, died: 06 Jan 2001, married to Jacob Lundsbjerg, male, born: 30 Jan 1920, died: 24 Jul 1995

i) Pól Jacob Lundsbjerg, male, born: 23 Aug 1941, married to Ranveig Andreasen, female, born: 12 Aug 1944

ii) Hansina Lundsbjerg, female, born: 03 Mar 1947, married to Sofus Baldwinson, male, born: 15 Apr 1944

d) Martin Jacobsen, male, born: 06 May 1920, died: Mar 2002, married to Nelly Hansen, female, born: 25 Jun 1921

i) Johannus M. Jacobsen, male, born: 03 Aug 1942, married to Irena Petersen, female, born: 18 Dec 1944

ii) Anna Margretha Jacobsen, aka: Dikkan, female, born: 30 Jul 1944, married to Albert Róin, male, born: 06 Aug 1936

iii) Alma Jacobsen, female, born: 27 Nov 1947, married to Poul Taabel, male, born: 12 Jul 1951

iv) Magnus Jacobsen, male, born: 12 Dec 1953, married to Pia Andersen, female, born: 19 Mar 1963

v) Elinborg Jacobsen, female, born: 07 Sep 1958, married to Ivan Højgaard, male, born: 19 Apr 1955

e) Esmann Jacobsen, male, born: 31 Mar 1922, died: 01 May 2002, married to Gunnleyg, female, born: 25 Feb 1931

i) Sigrun Jacobsen, female, born: 17 Oct 1955, married to Bogi Wardum, male, born: 31 Dec 1954

ii) Sigvør Jacobsen, female, born: 11 Nov 1962, married to Kristoffur Laksá, male, born: 26 Oct 1961

iii) Jóan Pauli Jacobsen, male, born: 30 Apr 1965, married to Joan Isaksen, female, born: 23 Jun 1966

THE MISSING SON — A FAROE ISLAND SAGA

- f) Johannes Marius Jacobsen, aka: Hanni, male, born: 20 Aug 1923, died: Jul 2002, married to Paula, female, born: 26 Oct 1925
    - i) Niels Jákup Kaj Jakobsen, male, born: 27 Nov 1948, married to Eva Erlandsdóttir, female, born: 04 Mar 1956
    - ii) Anna Katrin Jacobsen, female, born: 27 Oct 1950, married to Torstein Holm, male, born: 27 May 1945
    - iii) Johannes Pauli Jacobsen, aka: Lítli, male, born: 19 May 1952
- g) Sam Jacobsen, male, born: 21 Sep 1924, died: 06 Aug 1983, married to Margretha Guttesen, female, born: 26 Apr 1925, died: 14 Jul 1975
    - i) Johild Susanne Katrine Jacobsen, female, born: 02 Dec 1944, married to Ola Nicolajsen, male, Divorce
    - ii) Hjørdis Jacobsen, female, born: 30 Jun 1946, married to Høgni Danielsen, male, born: 27 Nov 1939
    - iii) Sam Jacobsen, male, born: 26 Feb 1948, married to Malan Hansen, female, born: 07 Jul 1950
    - iv) Maria Jacobsen, female, born: 13 Aug 1949, married to Hans Pauli Højgaard, male, born: 11 Mar 1946
    - v) Evert Jacobsen, male, born: 05 Aug 1952, married to Hjørdis Egholm, female, born: 20 Nov 1953
    - vi) Eiler Jacobsen, male, born: 23 Oct 1953, died: 29 Oct 1955
    - vii) Eiler Jacobsen, male, born: 26 Nov 1955, married to Jóna Hansen, female, born: 01 May 1956
      *2nd Wife of Johannes Pauli Jacobsen, Susanna Cathrina Danielsen, female, born: 02 Dec 1883, died: 18 Oct 1950

5) Joen Frederik Jacobsen, male, born: 01 Aug 1890, died: 10 Jan 1971, married to Malene Hansen, female, born: 01 Jul 1889, died: 29 Jun 1931
   - a) Anna Dagny Jacobsen, female, born: 24 Aug 1918, died: 07 Feb 1988, married to Jens Elias Hansen, male, born: 23 Feb 1912, died: 04 Oct 1984

APPENDIX II

    i)   Malena Hansen, female, born: 12 Jul 1939, married to Arthur Hansen, male, born: 03 Sep 1940

    ii)   Poul Birgir Hansen, male, born: 08 Feb 1941, died: 15 May 2003

b) Nikolina Jacobsen, aka: Ninna, female, born: 29 Dec 1919, married to Jens F. Poulsen, male, born: 24 Jun 1915, died: 26 Nov 1999

    i)   Henry Poulsen, male, born: 28 Feb 1942, married to Ellen Cemina, aka: Mina, female, born: 08 Jul 1943

    ii)   Símun Poulsen, male, born: 30 Sep 1947, married to Óluva Joensen, female, Divorce

        *2nd Wife of Símun Poulsen, Kára Lervig, female, born: 28 May 1946

c) Magdalena Jacobsen, female, born: 16 Aug 1922, died: Aug 1999, married to Børge Nielsen, male, born: Nov 1920, died: 1972

    i)   Jógvan Nielsen, male, born: 01 Apr 1961, married to Joan, female

    ii)   Erik Nielsen, male, born: 1967, died: Unknown

d) Petra Jacobsen, female, born: 18 Aug 1924, married to Sjúrður Hentze, male, born: 04 Jan 1921, died: 23 Sep 1998

    i)   Jógvan Hentze, male, born: 12 Aug 1954, married to Laura Justinussen, female, born: 03 Feb 1957

    ii)   Malfrið Hentze, female, born: 26 Aug 1955, married to Andreas M. Petersen, male, born: 09 Jul 1953

    iii)   Beinta Hentze, female, born: 10 Oct 1958, married to Torleif Justinussen, male, born: 18 Nov 1955

    iv)   Kjartan Hentze, male, born: 03 Apr 1966, married to Mildrid, female, born: 30 Jan 1968

e) Aksel Jacobsen, male, born: 29 Oct 1927, died: 05 Aug 2009, married to Ida, female, born: 16 Nov 1931

    i)   Jógvan í Lon Jacobsen, male, born: 14 Dec 1957, married to Andrea, female, born: 07 May 1957

    ii)   Inga Jacobsen, female, born: 09 Dec 1959, married to Jógvan Petersen, male

THE MISSING SON — A FAROE ISLAND SAGA

6) Sigga S. Magdalena Jacobsen, female, born: 28 Nov 1893, died: 12 Oct 1896

7) Hans Niels Peter Sophus Jacobsen, male, born: 01 Mar 1896, died: 28 Mar 1979, married to Susan Mildred Starns, female, born: 12 Aug 1902, died: 28 Jan 1997
   a) Peter Milton Jacobsen, male, born: 29 Nov 1942, married to Joanne Thomas, female, born: 10 Jul 1943
      i) Eric Thomas Jacobsen, male, born: 22 Sep 1965, married to Annette Dani Madruga, female, born: 04 Mar 1968, Divorce
         *2nd Wife of Eric Thomas Jacobsen, Fatima Topeta, female, Divorce
      ii) Jeffrey Jacobsen, male, born: 07 Aug 1967, married to Beth Marie Pieretti, female, born: 09 Mar 1963, Divorce
      iii) Russell Jacobsen, male, born: 16 Aug 1976, married to Shan Shan Liu, aka: Chloe, female, born: 21 Oct 1978
      iv) Kristopher Jacobsen, male, born: 27 Sep 1978, married to Elisabeth Jacobsen, female, born: 07 Jan 1982
   b) Jennifer Elizabeth Jacobsen, female, born: 25 Apr 1946, married to Curtis James Henke, male, born: 19 Jul 1945, died: 26 Nov 1999
      i) Jonathan Andrew Henke, male, born: 27 Mar 1972
      ii) Natasha Suzanne Henke, female, born: 22 Dec 1975, married to John Stanley Jacob, male, born: 06 May 1973

8) Adopted daughter Elsa Thomina Poulsen, female, born: 17 Jan 1904, died: 03 Sep 1997, married to Poul Reines, male, born: 13 Jan 1898, died: Feb 1957

Made in the USA
San Bernardino, CA
02 July 2018